Welcome to the Top

Secrets to Success from Leading Entrepreneurs

Second Edition

Monica Davis

An Atela Productions, Inc. Book

Copyright © 2020 by Monica Davis

Published in the United States of America by Atela Productions, Inc.

Visit us on the web at https://www.secretstosuccessbooks.com

ISBN: 978-1-7348699-2-7

Ebook ISBN: 978-1-7348699-3-4

Library of Congress Control Number: 2012955087

Second Edition

"Welcome to the Top puts business mastery at your fingertips. Learn the secrets of top CEOs and entrepreneurs that will help you quickly break through financial and business barriers to achieve unprecedented success."

— William R. Patterson, CEO, The Baron Solution Group, wealth coach and bestselling co-author of *The Baron Son*

"Welcome to the Top is filled with valuable stories and brilliant tips that will catapult entrepreneurs to leap forward to success. Each of the business owners in this book passionately shares their personal story including their honest to goodness mistakes. The wisdom they each share is profound and will shorten the learning curve for readers and save them from making a boatload of costly mistakes. Monica Davis' *Welcome to the Top* is a masterpiece and absolute must read for entrepreneurs and for those starting a business. This book should be mandatory reading in every business school."

— Chrissy Carew, Hall of Fame Master Certified Coach, founder, Insightful Player LLC, and author of *Insightful Player*

"Wow, I simply love this book. I couldn't put it down; each page was inspiring and led to the next. I love the fact that Monica Davis took the time to compile an impressive list of exceptional people and their empowering stories. I was empowered by this tome of collective wisdom and insights. *Welcome to the Top* is a must read for every Black American who is serious about leading a fulfilling and productive life. My heartfelt thanks go out to Monica for providing us a clear way to manifest our destiny."

— George C. Fraser, CEO, FraserNet, and author, *Success Runs in Our Race* and *CLICK*

"Monica Davis' *Welcome to the Top: Secrets to Success from Leading Entrepreneurs* proves once again that no matter from where you begin, you can reach the top! The path is made clear in this book by experts who provide information, how-to tips, and their own success stories to light the way. Ms. Davis interviewed countless entrepreneurs who had first-hand knowledge of the challenges and setbacks, near misses and successes. As an interviewer, she is like Diane Sawyer and Oprah Winfrey rolled into one. She not only gathered little-known facts and details about what makes entrepreneurs successful, she delved into their personal lives to find the secrets of character and perseverance that made the difference for them. Whether you are a solopreneur going it alone, an entrepreneur with staff, or a small business person *Welcome to the Top* can give your business a boost if you choose to put the secrets you find here into practice. This book belongs at the top of your list of must-read books."

— Jo Condrill, President, GoalMinds, Inc., recipient of the Ford Tribute to Business Women Leaders Award, and bestselling author of *101 Ways to Improve Your Communication Skills Instantly* and *Take Charge of Your Life*

"Welcome to the Top is a remarkable book for entrepreneurs, business owners and executives alike. Read it, apply it, and watch your business prosper."

— Dr. Patrick McNally, Ph.D., therapist and business strategist, and bestselling author of *How to Live an Amazing Life*

Table of Contents

Section 9: Inspiration and Self-Empowerment

Section 10: Other Success Stories

Preface

My goal in writing this book is to inform, educate, inspire, and provide invaluable resources to help you build your business in a way that will enable you to achieve the greatest amount of success in the shortest time possible.

This book features amazing success stories and articles collected from interviews with top business leaders, CEOs, industry experts, and entrepreneurs who have been featured in *Exceptional People Magazine*.

The personal stories in this book will give you ideas about the endless possibilities you can use to grow your business. Woven into these stories are advice and powerful insights to personal power, influence, and wealth.

The advice of these individuals is based on many years of proven experience. They know what works and what doesn't. They have helped thousands of success-minded individuals reach unlimited potential.

Acknowledgements

I will first thank my parents for preparing me to become independent by encouraging me to be confident, become an action taker and visionary, and be self-assured in my thinking, actions, and behavior.

Thank you to my sister Beatrice, who has supported me unconditionally as I began my journey as a magazine publisher. You have played an important role in the success of the publication since its inception.

Special thanks to all the guests whom I've had the pleasure of interviewing and featuring in *Exceptional People Magazine*. Thank you for sharing your personal stories and extraordinary business insights. They have inspired me, and I am thankful to have the opportunity to share them with my readers. Your stories have had an amazing impact on lives around the world.

Thank you to all my contributors and writers who have been an integral part of my endeavor to change the lives of thousands of people.

Thank you to Betsie Miklos whose generosity to help edit this book was a wonderful surprise.

I also thank all my readers. Without you, there would be no *Exceptional People Magazine*. I consider each of you to be exceptional in your own way.

Introduction

As I began writing this book, I reflected upon my life's mission which has remained unchanged since childhood. My life's purpose is to help others discover the best that is within them, guide them to reach their potential, and fulfill their vision in whatever they choose to do.

This book, although focused on business, is built on that premise. It provides resources and tools for professional and business growth. It also provides powerful insights to achieve that growth in a way that will save your most precious resources – your time and money.

This book shares essential components that can give you the power to create unlimited possibilities in your personal and professional life as well as your business. It will also help you develop a pattern of success and view your life and your business from a new perspective.

I thank you for taking the time to read this introduction and for exploring the pages that follow.

Using Keys to Gain Access to Unlimited Possibilities

Keys are made to give you access to things you ordinarily cannot access. The keys to success are not always evident. They come in many different forms. When you develop a mindset for growth, abundance, and prosperity, you'll learn how to identify keys to success that may often be hidden from others.

The keys to success can be presented to you in various ways, such as gaining information, meeting people, and even obtaining passwords. Integrity, hard work, and perseverance are also keys to success.

It is often said, "When one door closes, another opens." But in order for it to open, someone must be on the other side or you must have the key to unlock it.

Every day we each hold a set of keys that can unlock opportunities we never realized. At the end of every day, take time to think about the keys you were given and how you can use them to unlock doors of opportunity for yourself and share them with others.

This book is filled with keys that can help you achieve greater success in your business and professional career. I encourage you to use this information to recognize and unlock your true potential to achieve a lifetime of success.

"Success means we go to sleep at night
knowing that our talents and abilities were used
in a way that served others."

Marianne Williamson

Be Thankful and Pass It On

We are each blessed every day with the gifts of life, knowledge, talent, sight, hearing, and more. The list is much too long to mention.

We're also recipients of gifts from others such as friends and colleagues who give us ideas we didn't have before. They may give us an encouraging word when we least expect it, or they may lend a helping hand during hard times. These are all forms of gifts, and we must learn to recognize and appreciate them. It is never the size of the gift that matters, but the spirit in which it is given. Accept each gift with gratitude. It is not enough to receive and be thankful for life's gifts, but you must pass them on so that others may experience joy in their lives.

There is no gift too small. Small blessings often mean a lot. I encourage you to be a blessing to someone every day. Recognize and develop the talents you have as an individual and as a business owner and share them with others.

Believing Is Receiving

Though intangible, there's amazing power in the mind. Your mind is a resource that is more precious than any other resource on earth. It allows you to determine your own future. It gives you the power to change someone else's life. It will allow you to conceive ideas of gold and lead you to endless possibilities.

Do you believe you have the power to change your life? Do you believe you can achieve amazing success through your business? Almost everything that we see and touch comes from the power of the mind. Someone thought of it and they created the belief within them that they could make life better for others and for themselves.

What is your belief system?

If you believe in yourself, your abilities, and God-given talents and use them correctly, you shall reap the benefits. Believing is the first step to getting results.

Step Out Into the Unknown

Life is full of unknowns. This will always remain a constant. The fact that you made the bold decision to start a business means you have the courage to face many unknowns.

You've heard people say, "This is the way it's always been done. Why should we change it?" It is this kind of thinking that limits their true potential and success. I encourage you to break away from the status quo. Be bold. Step out of your comfort zone and fearlessly approach the unknown.

In a world that is changing more than ever before, doing "business as usual" can often lead to stagnation or a lack of intended results. You are remarkable. You have the power to use your mind to be creative, develop new ideas, and think well beyond the box.

Don't be limited by the thinking of others. Do not stagnate your own thinking. Explore new horizons and dream big.

The Mind

By Monica Davis

The Mind. A masterpiece when molded and
sculptured to focus on success.

The Mind. An ingenious tool;
when used constructively,
will allow you to conceive ideas of gold,
and lead you to endless possibilities.

The Mind. A state
that brings one to his knees in depression;
but allows the same one to be
elated with happiness.

The Mind. When refreshed,
can absorb enormous amounts of information,
but when fatigue sets in,
it reacts to words without comprehension.

The Mind. A time bomb
that when triggered by the evils of society, can
lead your body and soul to total destruction.

The Mind. An intangible source which lets you
choose your destiny.

How You Can Use This Book

Your success does not depend on what's happening in the economy. Your success solely depends on you. If you had the opportunity to talk to an expert about your business, what questions would you ask? You would probably ask questions that could help you learn the whys and hows of their successes and failures. You could also seek advice that would help you learn how to quickly expand and dramatically increase your bottom line while minimizing costly mistakes.

This is exactly what *Welcome to the Top* will do for you. This book includes extraordinary profiles and candid interviews with CEOs, award-winning experts, successful entrepreneurs, and professionals who dramatically changed their lives by following their passions and starting their own companies. Many started with nothing and have built multimillion-dollar businesses.

This book provides business solutions to your questions through riveting personal stories and experiences. Each story is filled with golden nuggets of wisdom and ideas that you can apply to your business and your life today. Even if your goal is not to become a multimillionaire, the lessons provided in this book can help you boost your bottom line and achieve extraordinary results.

Now you can learn their strategies and secrets. You can gain invaluable lessons from CEOs, celebrities, and everyday people who turned their ideas into multimillion-dollar entities. You can learn how to avoid the same mistakes they've made, apply many of their ideas and lessons to help you increase your sales, develop long-lasting business relationships, and build a remarkably successful business.

Welcome to the Top provides information to help you save two precious resources you can't afford to waste—your time and money. The information provided in this book can help you achieve your goals much faster while avoiding costly and unnecessary mistakes.

Gain first-hand advice from business icons like Tom Ziglar, CEO of the Zig Ziglar Corporation, who shares success insights that he employs every day to help open new doors of opportunity for hundreds of thousands of people. You will also gain invaluable wisdom from William R. Patterson, the number one wealth and business coach, who shares seven key elements to achieving wealth and business success.

These remarkable people candidly share the experiences and success strategies that they have applied to their own businesses. They talk about how they built their companies, how and why they decided to quit their jobs, and how to get and keep loyal customers. They share key elements to achieving overall success, how to effectively network and establish successful business connections, how to effectively negotiate to get what you want, and much more.

Each of them has many things in common with you. They didn't start out rich, but they had an idea. They all had an idea, a vision, and the belief they could become successful. Then they acted and became successful with a little hard work. They succeeded through trial and error and have graciously shared their experiences with me. Now I'm sharing many of their stories with you.

Your experience may not be exactly the same as theirs, but their life experiences can be used as proven examples as you pursue your business goals and dreams. Although each of them achieved success in their own way, their advice and wisdom will help you make better decisions. The lessons and insights you will gain from this book can provide you with a significant advantage by allowing you to do things better and faster.

Welcome to the Top can serve as a mentor to help you take your business to the next level.

Note: Throughout this book you will see bullets. These bullets identify specific information that I believe is of great importance as these experts and successful people share their powerful insights and advice. These insights helped them become mega-successful CEOs, entrepreneurs, and executives.

Although most of their experiences may not be related to your own, there are many lessons that can be gleaned from them to help you achieve success in your entrepreneurial endeavors.

Business Success

It's about more than just selling a product or service. Here are some examples.

Bama Does It Right

You may not have heard of The Bama Companies, but there's a 98% probability that you have bought one of their products. Have you ever tasted a hand-held pie, biscuit, donut, or pizza and immediately experienced taste buds full of goodness?

From pies to cakes to biscuits, it's perfection from the oven. Who's behind such delectable treats? The Bama Companies and its employees who believe in delivering perfection. At the center of such perfection is Paula Marshall-Chapman, CEO of the Bama Companies, Inc.

From the beginning, the main focus has been on quality and people. Bama Companies has come a long way from that small soda fountain in Texas to an enterprise that provides baked goods to several major food chains around the world. Specializing in hand-held pies, biscuits, and pizza crust, they have consistently delivered products that have tantalized the taste buds for over 80 years. Behind that great taste are people who care about quality and customer loyalty.

In order to produce and deliver high-quality products, you must have employees who believe in your mission and who are happy and satisfied with their performance and work. Whether you run a five-person company or a 5,000-person company, when your focus is on superior quality and great employees, the results will always be success.

Paula learned early on that a focus on quality and great people are what makes companies successful. These two ingredients are what Bama Companies was built on and has helped them maintain its superior level of achievement. They not only strive to build great relationships with suppliers but also with their employees.

As CEO, Paula is committed to giving back to her community and helping her employees become individual success stories while helping Bama maintain its iconic status in the commercial baking industry.

The Lesson: Anyone can deliver a product or service. What makes your service stand out? What will keep your customers coming back? Delivering quality products and services is an essential element to business success. Hiring employees who believe in your mission increases your ability to deliver high-quality goods and services because they are committed to your purpose.

The Golden Apple

Steve Jobs was a visionary, an innovator, and a pioneer who helped change the face of technology with the personal computer.

At an early age, he had an inquisitive mind—a mind for electronics, gadgetry, independence, and ingenuity that would later prove to change the lives of millions of prospective consumers. One day Steve Jobs shocked the world with his creativity and "dare to dream" perspective on life.

As co-founder of Apple Computers, Inc., in 1977 Jobs and Steve Wozniak created a masterpiece, The Apple II, which garnered over $150 million in sales in a three-year span.

The Macintosh computer introduced in 1984 also garnered some success but it did not catch on with businesses. Next, came a new computer called NeXT which targeted the educational market. It was known for its strong, object-oriented software development system, fast processing speed, graphic displays, and e-mail capabilities. However, the system did not quite catch on.

In 1986, Jobs purchased Pixar, formerly called The Graphics Group. It proved to be an extremely successful venture when it joined with Disney to produce several animated films, including the box office hit, *Toy Story*. Other films such as *Finding Nemo* and *The Incredibles* received Academy Awards for Best Animated Film. Pixar has now won 20 Academy Awards for its films.

From the Apple to the NeXT Computer to Pixar and back to Apple, Jobs' journey as a technological pioneer was an exciting ride, but it was not without setbacks. As motivational speaker Willie Jolley says, "A setback is a setup for a comeback."

Setting himself up for a comeback is exactly what Jobs did. After encountering business challenges with his ideas and inventions at various stages of his life, he refocused, repurposed himself, and reacted in a way that put Apple back on the map. As CEO of Apple, Jobs became a tough competitor in the computer industry.

Today, Apple boasts numerous successful products including the iPod, iPhone, iPad, MacBook, and many other products and services. It has become one of the most sought-after computer brands on the market and is also a leader in the digital music era due to the wisdom of Steve Jobs. No matter how you slice it, Apple is golden and its customers are biting into it worldwide.

The Lesson: Life is full of setbacks. When you encounter them, refocus, repurpose, and then react. You're surrounded by opportunities every day. Position yourself to be on the receiving end.

Envision It and Then Do It

For many years, Nike has redefined athletic footwear. You've seen the commercials, and you've seen the shoes on the feet of youngsters and adults alike. Who's at the helm of this sports authority? Mike Parker, president and CEO.

A company's success greatly depends on the working elements behind it. Designing the best athletic footwear and apparel is only a part of the equation. The company is focused on team building and incorporating strong independent minds from all backgrounds. These teams work together cohesively to envision and develop extraordinary growth strategies. Part of Nike's success is also attributed to providing outreach programs in America's communities and around the world.

The Lesson: Long-term business success is a culmination of total excellence derived from ethical values, excellent people who can help you broaden and expand your vision, and a commitment to quality, unique service, and social responsibility. A company's success is only as good as its leaders and the people it employs. Cultural diversity is an important aspect in ongoing growth. The most successful organizations get people to share their unique skills, experiences, and cultural knowledge.

Section 1

Strategies for Business Success

Key Tips for Operational Success

Entrepreneur Betsie Miklos, CEO of Miklos Systems, shares valuable lessons that she learned while building her business into a multimillion-dollar entity.

Trust and Respect! How Do You Run Your Company?

At an early age, it seemed that Betsie was destined for success. Not only had Betsie succeeded in a male-dominated industry, she obtained her mathematics degree in 1965 when it was an extraordinary achievement for women. In her own right, she has broken records.

As a young woman, she was introduced to computers when she worked for IBM, a company known to be in the forefront for women's equality in the 1960s. IBM presented opportunities that gave Betsie the foundation she needed to eventually start her business. During this period, she gained extensive experience while working with technically strong people who represented some of IBM's top clients. "I didn't think much about being a woman in a man's world," Betsie says.

Betsie's personal approach to work and business was strongly influenced by IBM's no-nonsense way of conducting business. These values included strong work ethics and nondiscriminatory policies. She always considered herself to be a team player who did her job well. Subsequently, Betsie assumed responsibility for establishing corporate culture and policies.

Betsie founded a software engineering company, Miklos Systems, Inc., which supports government contracts. She purposely chose not to go into a single-niche technology and took a deliberate approach not to hire individuals with limited expertise. "We want to hire people who are really good and have a wide diversity of computer skills," Betsie shares. "We want people who will grow, change, and work for their own growth."

Betsie created a training budget for her company because she understood the importance of employees expanding their horizons. "No one wants to do the same thing for 20 years. They want to grow and change." Miklos Systems encourages that kind of expansion.

Miklos Systems is family-oriented environment. Everyone is encouraged to learn and grow. Because of their varied backgrounds, employees are encouraged to seek assistance from each other when they encounter technical issues they can't resolve. Employees are also encouraged to consult with co-workers to learn more about specific technological areas prior to moving to new positions within the company.

After spending 10 years at home raising a family, Betsie returned to work for other companies, including TRW. She decided to become her own boss, and she began working for TRW as a contractor. She eventually became a one-person company, which she found to be very satisfying. Eventually, Betsie decided to expand her company. With expansion came the learning curve of bookkeeping, taxes, payroll, and the other necessities for running a business with multiple employees. Her approach to expanding Miklos Systems has been to keep growth at a slow rate of about two to four employees a year. "I watched a lot of companies grow very fast and not have the infrastructure in place to do it," she says. "You have to work to maintain the infrastructure as you grow."

A major reason for the success of Miklos Systems is that Betsie has hired employees that she likes being around, respects, and trusts. Most of the employees of Miklos Systems are from referrals, which have proven to be a great way to bring in top quality people.

- Betsie has intentionally never set goals for the company. She's never even done a five-year plan. "That doesn't mean we don't plan," Betsie states. "We have a business plan. We are adamant planners, but we take a different approach. We have contingency and back-up plans for everything that goes on in the company. We have thought through many contingences and what ifs, and we feel we are very prepared."

Miklos Systems has a low turnover rate—their retention rate is 98%. Out of the current 30 employees, seven are original employees, including Betsie, who have been with the company since 1996. Betsie says, "I don't know who gets credit for that, but I would like to think that it's the culture that we've formed here. [It's] basically [a culture that] respects people, supports them, and helps them find challenging work within the company." Betsie also offers the following advice for others who seek to start a business in the technology field:

- Stay current with technology. It is critical to invest in training for all personnel, both technical and office support. This is good for the individual and for the company. Keeping current with technological trends directly increases the knowledge base for your staff members and indirectly sends the message that you recognize and value each person.

- Get a good accountant and lawyer and make this part of your infrastructure. Setting up your books and legal documents correctly from day one pays benefits for many years. As a government contractor, Miklos Systems, is subject to government audits. Knowing everything is in order, as required, removes stress and anxiety.

- Surround yourself with people you respect and enjoy being around. It makes coming to work a lot easier.

- Know what your strengths and weaknesses are and make sure you hire qualified people you trust in your areas of weakness.

Betsie feels that one of her weaknesses is interviewing new employees. "I'm a terrible interviewer. I'm great at selling and explaining the company, but I like everybody I interview. It takes me two or three months of knowing a person to realize, "Oh! I missed that completely. It took me a long time to realize that about myself. I judge everybody very positively, and that is not a strength."

- Don't be afraid to fire a customer. There are some customers who cost you more than you get back from them. Of course, you don't want to approach the issue emotionally. Meet and talk with the customer and explain the problem you're having in a professional manner. It is a process.

- Try to balance your work and home life. Are you willing to hire others to offload work so you can buy yourself some time? Are you willing to bypass possible new business opportunities because the time required to write a proposal would mean having to work at night or weekends? Answering "Yes" to questions such as these demonstrates that balance is one of the core principles of Miklos Systems.

- Acknowledge the success of the company and its people through events and company celebrations. It may be an expense to the company, but it's well worth it to keep morale high and maintain great employees.

- Know your tolerance risk in relation to operating your business. How much debt are you willing to take on? How fast do you want to grow? It's very important to know your comfort level and to expand it slowly.

- Betsie's approach to business can be used as an exceptional guide for everyone who wants to follow their dreams of becoming an entrepreneur. Whether you want to start a technology company or a business in another field, many of the principles she has applied to her business can help you achieve success in your company. If your goal is to run a 100+ person company or a one-person business, preparation, trust, and respect will help you set a solid foundation for success.

Key Tips for Operational Success

Successful entrepreneur Sandra Pena, owner of Classic Hair Salon, shares business tips on what to look for when starting a new business.

A Style for Every Occasion

Before coming to California, I went to school in El Salvador to study cosmetology and got a job with a wonderful woman who believed in my abilities as a beautician. My family always wanted me to style their hair so it was natural for me to have a career as a beautician. Although it was a challenge, I did get my license.

When I first came to the U.S. from El Salvador, my country was in a civil war. I moved to Los Angeles, California for a while to begin a career in cosmetology. My years of experience have given me the ability to style any type of hair. I also style hairpieces for cancer patients and people with other hair problems.

After living in California for a few years, I decided to move to Virginia where I worked as a stylist in different salons for 24 years. Five years ago, I was presented with the perfect opportunity to start my own salon. I worked for a woman for two years who later decided to retire and sell her salon. She offered me the opportunity and I accepted. I felt it was the right time to move out on my own. I now own Classic Hair Salon.

I've owned my business for four years, and I've had many challenges including managing employees. The most difficult part early on was getting current employees to accept me as their boss after I bought the salon. The fact that I used to work with them as an employee made it hard.

I am proof that you can be successful no matter what your background is or where you come from. As long as you work hard and love what you do, you will do your best.

I've also worked as a cosmetology instructor for 13 years. My future goal is to own a beauty school, probably when I'm ready to retire. I love sharing my knowledge with aspiring beauticians. The most exciting part of teaching for me is watching students succeed at their craft. I get both a personal and financial satisfaction from being a hair stylist. Because of my desire to become an entrepreneur, I have accomplished a lot. Here are some of my tips for new entrepreneurs:

- Before you buy a business, get an expert who can advise you on what the process involves. You should also have an accountant and an attorney who will review your contracts before you sign them.

- Take courses in business management to learn how to run and manage your business.

- If you're buying a shop in a shopping center, make sure you contact the management about the type of signs you plan to use for the business. Some decisions are made by building management, not the county or city you reside in. There can be restrictions.

- Make sure you have the only business in your immediate area. Too much competition can hurt your business.

- It's better to have a corporation than a sole proprietorship because of tax purposes. Each has its tax advantages and disadvantages.

- You have to be strong but kind when managing employees. Be willing to train and share your knowledge with your employees. They will help your business grow.

14 Key Tips to Get Your Business Started

Successful entrepreneur Yvetta Drayton, The Sewing Diva, shares business tips and insights as well as her experiences as the owner her own company.

What was your inspiration for starting your own company?

When I moved to Loudoun County eight years ago, I noticed that there were a lot of young people here, but there were very few activities for them. I wanted to start a sewing school then, but it was not feasible at the time. Years later, when my work schedule changed, I started teaching sewing part-time in my home. When my work schedule changed again in spring 2006, I decided to take the plunge and pursue my dream of opening a sewing studio where people, both young and young at heart, could learn to sew. I wanted to empower others to unleash their creativity through sewing.

Describe your business.

The Sewing Diva operates The Studio of Fiber Arts. This school offers classes in garment sewing, home-décor sewing, quilting, knitting, and crocheting. The Sewing Diva also designs and fabricates custom window treatments and bedding.

What are some of your successes?

When I retired from my television job and transitioned into my business full time, I acquired students and clients immediately. One year later, I now have five great teachers and great classes for the summer.

My biggest successes are with my students. I believe that there is no point to sewing if the garment doesn't fit. I teach a fitting system that ensures the garment will fit the student. My students finish each project with a garment they can wear. They are excited about creating garments that look good and fit their bodies. This builds their confidence and encourages them to experiment with new techniques and styles.

Often ladies come with negative thoughts about their bodies and what they think they can't wear. I want ladies to develop a positive attitude about their bodies. When I show them styles that work with their body types and help them choose patterns, fabrics, and colors, they become excited about fashion, clothing, and sewing.

Share some of your failures and challenges and how you overcame or dealt with them.

One of my most recent failures was not being able to finish a creative project in a timely fashion. This situation was no one's fault, but it became everyone's problem. In the final analysis, I realized that I have the following weaknesses that must be worked on, including:

a. Researching the details and asking more questions

b. Creating a workable plan

c. Creating a realistic timeline, and

d. Discussing in detail exactly what will be required to do an excellent job

I love creating and designing. However, I am running a business and must weigh each project within those parameters. I am a perfectionist, and I am very meticulous. I need a certain amount of time and resources to do the job well. I love doing a great job. However, if certain aspects of the project prevent me from operating in a manner that is comfortable for me, I must be willing to say "No" graciously. When things don't work out, I try to always be gracious, even if I'm upset. Learn from it and move on.

What are the future goals and dreams for your company?

I plan to produce a website that allows anyone to play videos from classes at the studio. I want to produce a program about young people who sew. I worked in the television industry for many years, and I am excited about the possibility of adding this medium to my operations. I'd love to teach people to design their own clothes and produce a fashion show that showcases my students' talents.

What are some helpful tips and suggestions you can provide for other entrepreneurs?

- When you think about starting a business, focus on doing something you love, want to share, and don't need to take home.

- Clean up your credit and begin to lower your expenses.

- Attend seminars at your local small business development centers.

- Network with other business owners within your industry, both locally and globally.

- Even if you know your business and industry, continue with your education and get new certifications.

- Acquire an attorney, an insurance agent, and an accountant or CPA. This team will be your new best friends. Seek their advice and listen to it!

- Incorporate marketing and sales into your business plan. If you are not a marketing guru, find one immediately!

- Get a website.

- Listen to your clients, customers, and other successful business associates.

- Apply for business funding through SBA and your small-business development center.

- Use business contracts as much as possible. This is especially important with friends and family.

- Release yourself from unproductive people.

- Read *The E-Myth Revisited* and write down all of the jobs you perform in your business. When you begin to hire employees, you will know what skill sets your business needs and what job duties they will perform.

- Read the Bible daily. This has helped me treat everyone with respect and dignity, improve my awareness of certain problems that could occur in my business, and expand my ability to solve and cope with difficult situations.

*"Pretend that every single person
you meet has a sign around his or
her neck that says,
'Make me feel important.'
Not only will you succeed in sales,
you will succeed in life."*

Mary Kay Ash

Section 2

Sales and Marketing

6 Key Strategies to Dominate the Female Market

An award-winning sales expert, Judy Hoberman, author of *Selling in a Skirt*, shares her techniques on how to gain a larger female customer base.

A Sales Genie Outside the Bottle

With nearly 30 years of experience, Judy Hoberman is a natural-born leader in the sales arena. She knows what works and what doesn't. When it comes to selling to women, she has discovered sales techniques that outperform all others in her field. As an award-winning training director, Hoberman has shared her unique approach with audiences in the corporate and self-employment arenas.

Her book, *Selling in a Skirt*, reveals fresh, innovative ideas for men and women to identify distinctions in sales techniques between the genders. The book also provides advice on how to use these techniques to meet the demands of both large corporations and small entrepreneurs. No matter how many clients you have, you can always acquire more customers and additional sales.

Selling requires a unique combination of mindset and skills, and Hoberman has mastered them both. She has developed a female-focused approach and strategies that can help anyone gain additional clientele and a greater share of the market. If you're using an outdated approach to sales, then you're losing money.

Hoberman's 30 years of experience helps sales individuals and teams use a more savvy approach to selling. She has changed the way men think about their female counterparts in the business world because they now have an expert in their corner. Hoberman has graciously shared some of her invaluable business strategies with *Exceptional People* magazine. Check out her proven techniques in our interview below.

Monica: What are some common challenges that women face in sales?

Judy: Women like to build relationships, so the sales process can take a little bit longer. The number one challenge is time. Managers who don't recognize the importance of building relationships may feel that you're taking too much time. Sometimes the client thinks you're taking too much time, and your employer may feel the same way. Since women purchase 85% of all consumer products, they need to build customer relationships.

Monica: Can you identify some experiences you have had when being approached by a male salesperson?

Judy: I was going to lease a car, and I was deciding between two different vehicles. When I went to the first dealership, the salesman walked up to me and asked if I was going to buy a car that day. I said "Yes," and he brought me into his office and started filling out an application. I said, "You haven't even let me tell you what color car I want, let alone the questions I want to ask you."

When I said I had some questions, he rolled his eyes. At that moment, he lost a sale and didn't realize that he had lost it because he had not built a relationship with me. I was uncomfortable because I had questions, and I wasn't sure what I wanted. I asked him many questions, and he didn't change his attitude. It was not a favorable experience.

When I went to the second dealership, another gentleman came towards me, and he said something that changed everything. He told me that he knew buying a car is sometimes not a pleasant experience and he wanted to make it very pleasant for me. He asked, "What questions do you have, and how can I help you?"

It was like two opposite ends of the spectrum. The second man was so nice. I told him what happened earlier, and he said he was from a family of six sisters. He stated that he knew how women like to be treated and that's the way he treated them. It was a very pleasant experience that positively overshadowed the negative experience.

Monica: That's excellent. He understands where women are coming from.

Judy: Absolutely.

Monica: Why do you believe women are treated differently by salespersons and specifically by men?

Judy: It's not only by men. Sometimes women treat you differently as well. The problem that we faced for many years was that women in the workforce were hired in administrative support positions. They weren't hired in more responsible positions. I'm not saying that being in an administrative support position is not professional or admirable because it certainly is. It's really hard to do because you're helping to run an operation. At that point in time, women were not hired in sales and, if they were, they were among a small number.

For the first time in the United States, women constitute about 50% of the workforce. If you don't hire women, you're cutting your chances of being successful by 50%.

When I talk to people, I never say women are better "at this" or men are better "at that." I try to incorporate the differences that would make a powerful team and results in assets rather than liabilities. In the end, there should be no reason to hire a man over a female. You shouldn't have to hire females to simply meet a quota. That's when the resentment comes in. Women have to work ten times as hard as men to be taken seriously.

Monica: It's still happening today. What gender-based talents do women have that can be used to enhance their ability to become successful salespersons?

Judy: Building relationships. It's in our DNA. Women like to belong and build relationships. That's the number one quality. Generally speaking, we are in a society that has morphed away from being transactional (i.e., the way men did business) into being more relational (i.e., the way women generally do business). Women also have great instincts. Unfortunately, many times we don't follow our gut feelings.

When I was selling, I would say, "I don't understand why you're doing it this way. Why wouldn't you want to build a relationship and get referrals?" I was told that I was being a girl. They also challenged me on why I had to be friends with everyone and why I asked so many questions.

In the 90s when I was beginning in insurance, we didn't have computers. We worked using the yellow pages. That's where our leads were. We had to find ways to generate business. After about three or four months, my business was conducted solely on referrals because I had built relationships.

The person whom I reported to said, "It's great that you have all these referrals. I don't understand how you do it, but we're not going to use your system because it's not duplicable." In other words, it was not from a sales book. It's not like you can sit down with someone and say, "First you say this and then you say this." Building a relationship means asking the right questions and engaging in conversation.

Monica: You discovered an approach to sales that you are now helping companies and business owners to apply to their operations. What is your approach and how did you discover it?

Judy: It was all survival because whatever company I was with, I was always in sales. I was in male-dominated industries, and I had no mentor. You make it up as you go along. It was more trial and error. When things worked for me, I would try to incorporate them into the company I was with. I always told everybody to ask an open-ended question and start a dialogue. Eventually, people will open up to you.

Ask the right questions and listen. If you ask all the questions and you get all the answers, then the close is a natural process. Over the years, I never sold anyone anything, but I was the number one producer because I employed a technique. I would see everyone. I never sold anything over the phone. Why? If I couldn't help them, I would refer them to someone else, or I would say I can't help you now. I would get referrals from everybody, and I never wasted anyone's time.

If I couldn't make it better for you, I didn't show you anything else. If your plan was better, I would say, "Stay where you are." People would tell me, "You're on straight commission. You just talked yourself out of a sale." I would say, "Yes I did because it's not right for you." That's how I live my life. You don't hurt someone just to make a dollar. I would rather not make the money and keep them as a friend because they would refer me to someone else. I never had to worry about what I told somebody because it was always the truth.

Monica: Do you believe that anyone can become an effective salesperson?

Judy: Absolutely. The one thing you can't teach people is to think on their feet. You either have it or you don't. But you can definitely teach a person to sell. You can take someone who doesn't like people and make them a great salesperson because you're teaching them how to build a relationship, how to ask questions, and how to listen. That's all sales is. But you have to believe in your product. If you have something that you don't believe in, you can't be successful.

Monica: Is there's a way to recover a lost sale?

Judy: Yes. It depends on why you lost the sale. If you lost it because the person had no money, which is the hardest objection to overcome, you could always ask, "What would it take? How could we work together?"

If you lose a sale because someone doesn't like your product or they don't like you, you have to go back and try to massage it a little bit. I always make sure that once I've made the sale, I service it. Once you make the sale, that's just the beginning. You have to remain in contact with the person going forward.

If somebody loses a sale, maybe they didn't follow up, didn't return the phone call, or didn't answer a question. You can always go back in. Can you recover every sale? Absolutely not.

Monica: If I'm a woman trying to sell to another female, is there a difference between that versus selling to a male?

Judy: Men are more transactional. Remember that men like facts, figures, features, and benefits. When you're talking to a man, generally you need to talk more in bullet points than in stories. They want to get to the bottom line while women need to have you paint the picture with them in it. She wants to know how your product or service is going to affect her and everybody in her family.

If she's buying a car, you have to ask her, "How does this affect you?" "Will your kids be riding in the car?" and "Will you use it for business?" You have to paint that picture. When you put the person inside that picture, they become part of it. They see themselves in it, and they see how it works for them. That's just how women think.

Oftentimes, women are busy. If you are trying to sell your service to a company, they don't have time to hear the stories. You have to take your cue from the person that you're talking to because you may have to change that story and make bullet points for a woman as well.

Monica: Talk a little about your book, *Selling in a Skirt*.

Judy: I started writing down different sales tips. I think if someone had told me this, it would have helped. In my book, I talk about the things that would help a woman in sales. There's also a part that helps men. It discusses how to recruit, train, and talk to women as well as how to retain them. There's a lot of great information for men and women.

Monica: You speak to people in corporations and other large groups. What type of feedback do you receive?

Judy: I tell funny stories, and I provide information that they can take away. Often they will say, "I can use this today. You just helped me. Now I can talk to my wife." When I speak, it's very light-hearted. I use my experiences to make a point. People walk away with at least one point that they can use that day.

Monica: Generally speaking, what are some key elements to developing an effective sales strategy?

Judy: It's all about the kinds of questions that you ask. It's also about the way you listen. There's nothing else to sales. I don't care what you sell or how expensive it is. If you don't ask the right questions and you don't listen, it doesn't matter if you're selling something for a penny or a million dollars. It doesn't matter how good a salesperson you are.

If you don't ask the right questions, you're not going to get anywhere. That's the simplest strategy I can give you. It's all about asking questions. There are different types of questions and there are different ways of thinking about the questions you ask, but it's all about the questions.

Monica: Would you recommend courses to anyone who is thinking of going into sales?

Judy: I always think that you should invest in yourself because times have changed. It doesn't matter how seasoned you are. When I first started in sales, there was no such thing as building a relationship. I did it because that's what felt good to me. But honestly, anything that you learned back in the 70s or 80s, they're really not incorporating anymore.

There are fabulous trainers with really good information, but you have to take that information and rework it into a relational activity. If you don't take some type of course every so often, you're going to lose some of the more recent ideas. If you can keep up with what's going on in the world, you'll be OK, but it's always good to invest in yourself. I always tell people to get a business coach. If you can afford one, you can't afford not to have one. They will keep you in line and keep you accountable.

Monica: Is there anything else that you'd like to mention?

Judy: Many people think that because the title of my book is *Selling in a Skirt* that I only work with women. It's not true. I definitely work with men. Many times, my audiences are 75% male.

One of the things I always say is that women like to be treated equally, not identically. Treat them equally and everything will work out. If you take the differences, understand them, and implement them, whether you're male or female, just imagine how powerful your team would be. It's all about figuring out how to make these differences work.

Monica: I would imagine a number of men listen to you speak because they are interested in bringing in more female customers. This has been a pleasure because it has been very enlightening for me, and I wish you all the success in the world.

Judy: I always make a bold promise. I promise you that your bottom line will go up when you incorporate what I tell you— NOT if, but when.

I also tell people that no matter how many questions I ask, I always ask the following question last: "Is there anything else?" I will tell you that all the times I've trained men, once I asked that question they would cringe. They would think "Oh, no. We're in for another hour." I want to know everything up front.

If I ask you, "Is there anything else?" and you said, "Yes," we continue our conversation. If I ask, "Is there anything else?" and you said, "No," then we're ready to close. We've had our conversation, and you've told me everything I need to know. The only thing left is to close.

I would never have to say, "Now give me a check," because they would say, "How do we do this? How do we get this going?" Don't be afraid to ask that last question. With that said, women still have to be able to close because that's the whole idea. You can't just visit forever and never make a sale, because that's not a good thing either.

Monica: Based on your experience, do you find that women have a hard time doing that?

Judy: Not all women. However, some women really just want to be friends, and they forget that they're there for a reason.

Monica: When you arrive at the point that you know it's time to close, is there a specific way you should ask for the sale?

Judy: You just say, "Now getting back to the cell phone program we're trying to put together for you, is there anything else that you need to know about it?" Whatever the product or service is, just go back and say, for example, "I believe I've answered all your questions. Is there anything else you need to know about how the cell phone works?" Bring it right back to that product or service. It puts you back on track.

Monica: Your advice is definitely sound.

"The ability to convert ideas to things is the secret to outward success."

Henry Ward Beecher

Section 3

43

Customer Service and Loyalty

What You Need to Do to Keep Happy Customers?

Rich van Engers, CEO of Sturdi Products, a leading pet carrier manufacturer, shares his experience of going from broke and divorced to becoming the CEO of a billion-dollar company. He also shares the one key element necessary for attracting and keeping happy customers—the same key element he uses each year to increase his profits.

A Stellar Reputation for Customer Service

It's been 19 years since Rich van Engers discovered what is now the most popular innovative design for pet carriers. Over the years, his SturdiBag brand has become the preferred pet carrier for professional trainers, breeders, and animal lovers worldwide. His family-owned company, Sturdi Products, has gained a stellar international reputation for designing durable yet uniquely attractive products for cats and small dogs.

Seventeen years ago, van Engers embarked upon this new endeavor. Here's a question: What would you say is the most important element when starting a new business? One might say market research. This is true, but in van Engers' case, he defied the norm and became a successful entrepreneur and business owner. He didn't know anything about market research, but he poured his heart and soul into making a product that he believed would meet a particular need.

"I was recently divorced. I was dead broke. I was riding my bicycle to work when one day I saw somebody with his arms wrapped around this box, struggling with a cat falling through the bottom. At the same time, I see this canvas awning coming off this building," van Engers says. Who would have thought that a cat falling out of a box and a canvas awning would change the pet carrier industry? It was that instance of inspiration that changed his life.

With no market research, how did van Engers survive and eventually beat the competition? He constantly develops, tests, and enhances his product. But more importantly, he listens to his customers and meets their needs.

He now realizes that market research is important and necessary to start any business. From his living room floor to an enormous warehouse, van Engers built his brand through hard work and word-of-mouth recommendations.

The founder of *Exceptional People Magazine* was thrilled to speak with van Engers about his business venture, his setbacks, and his success. Our interview begins here.

Monica: Tell me about your company, how you got started, and why you chose the pet industry.

Rich: It's a funny story actually. In 1993, I was recently divorced, and I was completely broke. I was riding my bicycle to work, and I was working for a major trucking company. One day I was driving past a veterinarian's shop and I see somebody coming up with their arms wrapped around this box, struggling with a cat falling through the bottom.

At the same time, I saw a canvas awning coming of a building, and I thought, "There has to be a better idea. There has to be a better way to do this."

So, I went to a friend who sews and told her, "I've got this idea for this new product. Do you want to help me sew and start a company?"

She said, "No, I'll show you how to sew, but I don't have time."

She let me use her sewing machine and showed me how to wind the bobbin. I went home, sat on the floor, and started cutting and sewing. I did the best I could. Then, I took it to a professional pattern maker and they made a couple patterns for me.

At that time, it cost me about a week's pay to have one prototype made. After I had a few more prototypes made, I put an ad in the paper for home sewers. Many people responded, but I only kept one person over the years. I cut the material, the webbing, and the notions, and then I would deliver everything to her.

Monica: What was the material?

Rich: At that time, it was 420-denier nylon. I had that idea of the awning in mind. I tried to sew it myself, but when I started working with the pattern maker, things changed a little, and we came up with the design. I had boxes in my living room with different pieces that would go into the pet carrier. I had 20 pet carriers made.

Monica: So that's what started it all?

Rich: This actually took a couple of years. From the time that I had the idea to sitting down and trying to sew it myself to sourcing raw materials to finding everything that goes into it to finding a decent name for the product.

Once I went to a cat show in Bremerton, Washington. I set 20 SturdiBags on the table and everything sold. I was blown away. I remember three Japanese women who, to this day, hug me when they see me; they bought two carriers each. I walked away with an empty table and $1,000 in my pocket. I also had many ideas from so many people. They would come by and they'd look at the product and say, "Boy, this is really great, but can you add a shoulder strap?" or "Can you add some kind of a flap or cover over the mesh?" With that first $1,000, I went back to the drawing board, put those covers over the mesh, added a shoulder strap on, and did what the people asked. I didn't know that I would see the same people at all the cat shows.

A couple of weeks later, I went to another cat show, and saw the same people. They came by and said, "Boy, you really listen to your customers."

It was then that a light went off. If you listen to your customers, you take care of them, you design what they want, and you include them in the design process. It's really a no-brainer. It's a simple way to do business. Listen to your customers.

Monica: You started this project without researching the market to see what was already out there.

Rich: I had no idea then. It's kind of a crazy way to do business. I had no idea what was on the market. When I showed up at the cat show, there was nothing like it on the market. At that time, there was only one soft carrier, which I learned later was the

Sherpa bag. It had one product. Years later, people would try to trade theirs in for one of ours because our bag is sturdy, flexible, lightweight, and easy to use. It's evolved over the years.

Monica: What is the major difference between your pet bags in comparison to what other companies are selling?

Rich: First, our bag is the only soft-sided pet carrier that has a patent. The reason it has a patent is because it has a flexible frame which allows it to conform into any small or tight space, such as an airline seat. Initially, nine-inch plastic boxes were being made to go under an airline seat. When I came up with the 12-inch SturdiBag, it was actually too big to fit under the seat. But when you pushed it down, it became a spring bag. That really set it apart. Going from cat show to cat show, there were so many suggestions. People would ask, "Can I seatbelt it into my car?" or "Can I tie it down on my bicycle?" To this day we have a reputation for listening to our customers. That's how we've developed more than 40 products over the years.

Monica: What are some other products that you have developed?

Rich: We have a pop-up shelter, which if you ever go to a cat show, we probably have 90 percent of the market share. The pop-up shelter is actually a soft-sided kennel. When you take it out of the bag, you give it a shake and it sets itself up. There's no assembly at all. We have different models, sizes, colors, and door styles. When we produce them for the European market, we create a vinyl window in the back for spectator viewing. We also make a larger one for the German market. We've had people in wheelchairs tell us that they hadn't been able to set up their own cage until we came up with this product.

Monica: What were some of the challenges you encountered in designing your SturdiBag and how did you overcome them?

Rich: Our main challenge was sourcing raw materials. There was nothing like it on the market and so everything that I needed, I had to find. It wasn't conventional. I couldn't go to a hardware store to find what I needed. I couldn't go to a fabric store, either.

Now we have a company that sources for us. But I always keep trying to improve. Since day one, that's what I've done. If I can improve the product, I will. With our warranty, it's imperative that we continue improving our product and make the best product we possibly can. The Sturdi Products label is an assurance of quality and innovation.

Monica: What would you say to other business owners and entrepreneurs about the importance of listening to their customers?

Rich: Business is really simple—you listen to your customers and do the right thing. Stand behind your products, take care of your customers, and make a product that people want.

Monica: Are your products mainly for cats?

Rich: Not necessarily. There are lots of dog users who use our products. Cavalier King Charles owners swear by Sturdi Products for small dogs. If you go to a dog show, maybe 10% of the dogs will fit into a SturdiBag, but if you go to a cat show, 100% of the cats will fit into a SturdiBag.

Monica: You've been in business for over 17 years. What do you attribute to the success of your company?

Rich: As I said, listen to your customer, offer excellent customer service, and continue to innovate and improve your products. We have many loyal customers who have been with us for years, and they feel like family.

Monica: You have done such an excellent job in building your company.

Rich: I'm very lucky and the reason is our customers. You include your customers, and you listen to them. If your customers have a problem with something, you treat that product like it's your very own.

With our customer service, we don't let people go to recordings. We answer the phone every time. We pride ourselves on it. I don't answer the phone very often, but if anybody ever wants to talk to me, they're more than welcome. I give them my direct line.

Monica: Sturdi Products is a family business. What kind of challenges have you encountered by hiring family members?

Rich: It's easier to hire them than it is to fire them. It just goes with our philosophy. You just treat people right. My parents were born in Indonesia. They were hardworking people. They left Indonesia right after World War II. They immigrated to the Netherlands where I was born.

After the Netherlands, they came to the United States. My father tried to get a job with Shell Oil. He had worked for Shell Oil in Indonesia where he had 5,000 people working for him. When he came here, he was told that he was too old. So he started washing dishes and he changed tires on cars just to feed the family. My son is also a very hard worker. We come by it honestly. We welcome input from everybody. My brother worked for me in Europe. My brothers have worked for me here almost 10 years. My son helped me get started years ago. It does make it nice to have your family around.

Monica: What do you find most rewarding about operating your business?

Rich: Seeing my product all over the world. When I first started this, I made 20 carriers. The first store I ever put my product in was in Amber, Washington. That little store bought two carriers from me. In the evening, when they were closed, I would stand in front of their window and look at my product and say, "OK, that's one store."

Now we're in thousands of countries all over the world. We send full containers to Russia, Germany, France, Italy, and Japan. We just began exporting to Beijing and Shanghai, which is just phenomenal for us because they typically knock off our products. They often copy our products in Russia and China.

Monica: There's really no way that you can control that.

Rich: No. What we do is we make a bigger presence. That's one of the reasons we're going to visit Russia. We did a special production run of Sturdi Products. We print our own materials. I buy raw goods in white, and then I have them printed. We've got thousands of prints to choose from, so there's no way that the companies that are trying to knock us off can keep up. By the time they knock off one of our products, we've already changed.

I picked up a couple of imitation products at the Global Pet Expo in Orlando I attended a few weeks ago. There was a Chinese company that had an imitation of one of my products with its label on them. I brought the products home and discovered that they're completely inferior.

One of the difficult things when I started this was sourcing materials. That's one thing they can't do. They may be able to copy the pattern, but they don't know where we get our supplies. For example, we use a specially produced material to make our rods that make our products flexible.

In the early days, there were problems with rod breakage. Now, we have them produced for us to our specifications in a factory where I can walk through and watch these materials being made. The people who are copying our products can't compete with that. They're trying to find cheap products and get them on the market as cheaply as they can.

With my products, I see some carriers that are 10-15 years old and they still look new. If somebody comes to us with an old product, we'll refurbish it for them at no cost.

Monica: How important is packaging?

Rich: It wasn't important in the early days because we were just selling them at cat shows. But now that we're in the megastores, packaging is very important. We've learned as we've gone along why some packaging will work and others won't.

Since we have so many colors, it's important for our customers to see the product through the packaging. They need to be able to open it, touch it, and seal it back again. That's one of the reasons we make our own packaging.

Monica: What are some stores in which your products are carried?

Rich: Petco, PetSmart, and Pet Travel. They're also huge in Europe.

Monica: What tips can you give consumers about selecting the best carrier? What should they look for when they are selecting a carrier for their pets?

Rich: We tell people that it should be as comfortable for you as it is your pet. You don't want to get anything that's too heavy or too bulky. Obviously, your cat or dog has to be comfortable and be able to get in and turn around. They usually don't stand up when they're traveling. You don't want anything too small for them, and most importantly, it should be comfortable for you. A cat or dog is going to adjust to almost any space. They're going to be happy as long as they're with you. But if you have a big, heavy, or cumbersome carrier and you're trying to go down the aisles of an airliner, it's not very simple.

That's why we try to make things as light as possible. We have a carrier that weighs three pounds but can hold a pet up to 40 pounds and retains its shape. If it's too large to fit under the seat, you just push it down, slide it under your seat, let go, and it springs back. You can utilize all the space under the seat.

Monica: What is the make-up of your customers? I would imagine they're all ages and backgrounds and from all walks of life.

Rich: We've seen everyone from children to people in wheelchairs. I've seen people in wheelchairs coming into shows and carrying our products on their wheelchairs.

Monica: Many entrepreneurs have ideas about creating a new product that they believe will fill a potential need. From your perspective, what steps should be taken to turn those ideas into reality?

Rich: Start with some research. Go to trade shows in that field and see what's already on the market. It doesn't make sense to produce something that someone else is marketing already.

A little bit of research can go a long way. That's something I didn't do in the beginning. I didn't know any better. Ignorance is bliss. Everybody has a great idea. Everybody has at least one great idea. It's just a matter of what they do with it and whether they follow through or not.

Monica: What are some things that you're working on for the future?

Rich: Wheels for our carriers. We just came out with our newest pet carrier, which we call the Incognito. It's upscale and has nice handles on it. We took it to a cat show and tested it in our market. We told them it wasn't for sale but asked, "What do you think about it?" They put their cats in it, tried it out, and just like the other shows, they gave us their input. Then we went back to the drawing board, changed it a little bit, and now we have it in production.

We also create SturdiBoxes. They are collapsible boxes that hold water and anything else you can think of. We make them in five different sizes, from two cups to five gallons. They're foldable, flexible, and easy to store. Backpackers use them to wash dishes. There are hundreds of uses for these things. You can store ice and cool drinks. There's no seepage whatsoever.

Monica: Thank you for the opportunity to learn more about Sturdi Products. With 17 years of great success, you're obviously doing the right things.

Rich: We owe it to our customers. Our customers are our best salespeople. It's really quite wonderful. We're blessed.

Monica: It's amazing that you have practically built your company just by word of mouth.

Rich: Word of mouth and no market research. That's why I stressed in the beginning that I was riding a bicycle.

Monica: I'm sure when you were riding that bicycle you never thought that you would achieve so much success.

Rich: No, I really didn't. I knew I had a good idea, but every day it just amazes me that we get calls from all over the world, from The Ukraine to exporting products to China. This is just phenomenal for me. I get to travel a lot. I meet distributors and customers. If there's an issue, if somebody has a problem with my products, I'll go there in person.

Monica: That's unheard of.

Rich: It really is. Nobody does that. Our customers built our company. If we don't take care of them, what do we have? The question becomes, "How long do you want to be in business?"

Do you want to be in business for two years, or do you want to stay in business and be able to pass it down to your family?"

53

5 Surefire Steps to Gaining Customer Loyalty

There's much more to customer service than simply providing them with a quality product. They may be happy with your product or service, but it doesn't mean they won't buy a similar product or service from your competitor. Customer satisfaction doesn't always lead to customer loyalty.

To gain customer loyalty you must go beyond providing them with a great product or even providing faster service. You must establish long-term relationships with them on a personal level. Build a rapport, take the time to learn about them, and understand who they are.

In a nutshell, to retain your current customers and improve sales, you need to develop a bond that will make your customers love you and the way you do business with them. Providing faster service or using more technology is not necessarily the answer. The use of technology these days, such as e-mail and voicemail, is often viewed as an impersonal way to communicate. It is necessary to consider other ways to keep your customers happy and help them become loyal customers.

Here are a few proven tips to help you go well beyond just customer service.

1. Build a Relationship with Your Customer

When I was working as a computer specialist, I learned to gain customer loyalty. As a result, I was the main focal point for helping high-level officials make important decisions that affected policy. Whenever there was a technological need, large or small, I was asked to be involved.

In addition to providing them with excellent service, I talked to my customers about their interests. I carefully listened to their needs and their wants. This is how you build a relationship with them. You can offer them compliments when appropriate and ask them how their day is going. It tells them that you are interested in them as a person, not just a means to an income.

2. Keep a Positive Attitude

If you're in a business that requires customers to visit your location, keep a positive attitude even when you're having a bad day. We all have bad days, but we shouldn't let them affect our customers. How we choose to deal with negative situations determines our mood and our customer's mood. A positive attitude can be contagious. Don't let them see you upset.

Always keep an upbeat attitude and provide service with a smile. If your customer is having a bad day, find encouraging words to brighten their day or put a smile on their face. They will remember you for your positive attitude.

Use humor—good clean humor—to break down any barriers. People like to laugh and if you can get your customers to laugh with you, you have formed an instant bond.

3. Show Concern

Take time to listen to your customers. Listening means understanding your client's needs. Give them your full attention and make them feel important. Ask open-ended, follow-up questions that allow them to open up more. Show them that you care about their situation.

4. Make Them Feel Like Family

If you've taken the time to build a relationship with your customers by listening to them, you'll be surprised how much you can learn about them as they share their lives with you.

A great way to create customer loyalty is to remember special days in their lives, such as birthdays or their child's graduation. Ask them about a recent event they told you about or inquire about a recent illness they may have mentioned. By remembering something personal about your customers, you will stand out from all the others who don't.

5. Offer Creative Solutions, Even if They Don't Ask

Another great way to gain the loyalty of your customers is to go beyond providing them the product or service they requested.

Offer ways to help them avoid common mistakes or major catastrophes. Don't wait for them to ask. Show them how they can use the product or service more efficiently. If you know there are things they can do with the product to help make their lives easier, share that advice with them.

As a computer specialist and software engineer, I never hesitated to show my customers more efficient ways of doing business to help them eliminate extra steps or avoid making costly mistakes within their business processes. Everyone wants to save time and money when they can. I helped them improve their workflow. Use this approach in your business and watch your customers come back again and again.

Section 4

Networking and Relationships

3 Dominant Keys to Build Valued Business Relationships

Networking guru George Fraser, CEO of FraserNet, Inc., shares three key elements to building valued business relationships and principles to change your life.

World's Foremost Networking Expert

Online social networking is the latest craze with many millions of people joining in. From Facebook to Twitter to LinkedIn, social networking has become the "in" thing. So what happened to the personal touch and meeting in a room filled with individuals?

Building successful relationships at organized functions has existed for many years and it remains one of the most effective ways to build a network of contacts. Who knows that better than one of the world's greatest networking gurus George Fraser?

Born and raised in a family of 11 children, Fraser's childhood was not what most kids dream about—a carefree life with friends and playful times to remember. Instead, at the age of three, he and his siblings were orphaned, separated, and placed in foster homes. His mother became mentally ill and because his father lacked the education needed to get a higher paying job, he could not handle the responsibility of 11 children. Driving a cab 12 to 14 hours a day was not enough to support his family.

"It is not where you start, but where you finish," says Fraser. Even as a young child, he wanted more out of life. Self-preservation was on his mind. He wanted to escape the rough, mean streets of New York and the foster homes in which he and his siblings resided.

You can grow up in a wonderful home, but if you allow the external and negative forces of your environment to change your view of life, you will not become productive as an adult. If you didn't succeed in your endeavors as a child, that doesn't have to affect the remainder of your life. Despite an unkind childhood, Fraser has achieved an amazing level of success, and he is now helping thousands of people to develop successful businesses and professional relationships.

He is often called "America's networking guru." Through years of perfecting his craft, Fraser has built a company that provides thousands of people with the elements essential to successful networking. His annual Power Networking Conference draws over 40,000 attendees.

Early in Fraser's career, he realized that he had a skill only a few possessed—the ability to establish and nurture successful relationships. Fraser shared with *Exceptional People Magazine* how he went from an unpleasant childhood to a life of success through hard work, commitment, and integrity.

Monica: You had a very interesting childhood, and I would like you to provide some insight into what your childhood was like.

George: I was born and raised in Brooklyn, New York in a family of eleven children—eight boys and three girls. My father came to this country in the early 1900s from Guyana. He married a beautiful, fair-skinned sister, Ida Mae Baldwin from Lumpkin, Georgia, and they lived in Brooklyn.

When I turned three years old, my mother became mentally ill and was institutionalized for the balance of her life. My father, as a black man, could not get a good education and a good job in the early 1900s in America. Relegated to driving a New York City cab, he had to work 12 to 14 hours a day and could not care for eleven children, so we were orphaned. I stayed in an orphanage from age three to five. No one would take eleven children, so we were broken up into threes. Until I aged out of foster homes, I spent the balance of my young life growing up on the mean streets of New York.

It was a very tough life. It's not an indictment of the foster homes. It is just that the foster homes where I was placed were very toxic. I aged out at 17. Aging out simply means that the foster parents are not paid for your care. They either volunteer to keep you or you have to leave. In my case, I had to leave.

I went back to the brownstone my father maintained while we were in foster homes. There I was met by several of my older brothers who had aged out as well. The difference between us was that they were heroin addicts living a very toxic life, and I was 17 years old in a bad environment. I understood very deeply that I would have to get out of that environment or I would probably end up like them.

Monica: How did you escape from the negative environment of the streets that overtook your brothers?

George: We lived in different foster homes. The foster home in which I was placed was in Queens, New York. I was not exposed to the street life they were exposed to. It was a much more innocent lifestyle. I was nurtured differently than my brothers. So that's how I escaped. It was a little bit of luck, a little bit of nature, and some nurturing.

As soon as I was able, I packed my bags and took a Greyhound bus to Cleveland, Ohio where my older sister, who was a nurse, took me in. I didn't report back to my family for five years to let them know where I was. I didn't want my family to know where I was until I got my life together. When I got my life together, I went back to New York and I saved two of them.

While in high school, I was shipped off to a vocational school. I obtained a vocational diploma in woodworking from Thomas Edison High School because no one thought I was college material. I didn't agree. For several years, I worked the midnight shift at LaGuardia Airport mopping floors to pay my way through college, disproving what people believed about me.

The motto of that story is very simple. It is not where you start, it's where you finish. That's the big lesson that I teach and preach to people. You can grow up in dire circumstances and in spite of those circumstances, you can excel. You can do well if you follow certain principles and rules in life.

When I was growing up, divorce among our people was certainly not what it is today. Our families stayed together, come hell or high water. My father, in spite of the fact that my mother was in a mental institution for the remainder of her life, never remarried. He stayed connected to her and kept us connected to her. We went to visit her in the mental institution. She hardly recognized us. She was basically insane. We returned home when we were older, able to care for ourselves, and earn our own way.

Everybody has a story. The question is, "Are you willing to analyze and understand who you are, why you are, and the motivating factors that you need to succeed?" My motivating factor was I wanted to escape. I wanted to escape my circumstances. I wanted more than what I had been exposed to.

Monica: Would you say your past experiences have had an impact on your 36-year marriage?

George: Absolutely. I had a father who had a mentally ill wife who was institutionalized, but he stayed married to her until they died. I had foster parents who stayed married until they both died. Those were my models, and that model simply said that life isn't a crystal staircase. We're all human. We all bring baggage to the table of life. We all have our issues, challenges, and differences.

How can I grow up in one environment, you grow up in another, and when we get married, how could someone expect us to be exactly the same? There are going to be differences, but you live through those differences. You iron them out and you stay together for the sake of family, community, and children. That's the kind of environment that I grew up in. That's the kind of environment that we need to get back to today.

Monica: When did you realize that focusing on networking and bringing people together was your calling?

George: It came to me during the middle of my life. After spending nearly 20 years working in the public and private sectors as an executive with Proctor and Gamble, United Way, and Ford Motor Company with only a vocational high school education, I outperformed and achieved more than most of the people around me who graduated from Harvard, Morehouse, Yale, and Dartmouth.

I was being promoted and achieving extraordinary results wherever I worked. It wasn't because I was the smartest person in the room or had the most illustrious credentials. What I noticed was that I had the best interpersonal and people skills.

My emotional quotient and my ability to cultivate, nurture, and build relations were far superior to the people around me.

I had skills and I learned the jobs that I was assigned. I developed my skills around the responsibilities that I was given. I had the raw talent. I just didn't have the formal education. What I had that was better than most were relationship-building skills. I knew when to lead and I knew when to follow. I knew how to love and like people and how to have them love and like me.

I kept asking myself, "I wonder if black people understand how important this relationship-building skill is in their climb and in their success?" I began taking a harder look at that. I began speaking on it while I was employed. Then I decided that I would leave the velvet handcuffs of my six-figure salary and start a business teaching culturally specific communities about the power and importance of relationships.

I didn't invent the science. The science was invented by white people. White people have been doing this effectively for many years. It's something they never talk about. It's something they just do. Jewish people don't have networking meetings and training. They just do it. It was my personal life, my personal revelation, my personal analysis on why I was succeeding over so many of my friends and colleagues.

The first business I started was called Success Source: Linking People and Ideas. I funded it with my stock options from Proctor and Gamble. The first product that I produced for Success Source was a series of monthly networking events called *Success Net: Success Through Networking.*

It was a brand-new concept no one had ever seen before. In fact, it hadn't been done anywhere in the country. It was simply inviting African American professionals, leaders, and business owners to a venue. The first hour was cocktails and then I taught people how to engage in conversation and exchange business cards. I brought in well-known speakers such as John Johnson from *Ebony* magazine and Ron Brown who was then chairman of the Democratic Party. That's how *Success Net* began. We named it "The Party with a Purpose."

Monica: You have built a global network of 40,000+ people who meet annually. Did you think you would accomplish something so large?

George: Quite frankly, no. I wasn't thinking that far in advance. I live by a very simple philosophy—first things first, second things never. Do the first thing—what's in front of you. Do it with excellence. Do it with quality and then the second thing will be first and you focus on that. It's no different than climbing a mountain. You have to climb the mountain looking at the first step right in front of you. You have to look down to climb up.

I've always lived by that philosophy. I put on an excellent program and I got people totally excited about my ideas. Then you put on the next program and more people will become excited. If you just keep doing that, before you know it, you'll be at the top of the mountain and that's exactly what happened. You have to be patient because you cannot run up a mountain. It takes planning, time, and focus.

Monica: How many years did it take to build your business to the point where you have many people who attend annually?

George: It took 20 years and 250 events. This is before the Internet. Therein lies another lesson. Chart a good and righteous course and stay that course. You have to know what is right for you, begin down the path, and stick with it. If you do that, it will be impossible to fail.

Monica: What are your thoughts on the Internet and social networking?

George: I think it's wonderful. However, it needs to be used in a specific way, especially if you're in business. It's very helpful, especially for people who are shy. It's a great way to meet new people all over the world. Here's the caution—it cannot replace face-to-face meetings. It cannot replace the human spirit, the human voice, and the human touch. At some point in time you're going to have to get out of your bunny slippers, get out of your pajamas, get your hair done, and come out into the real world. You have to talk to, meet with, and greet people. You have to press the flesh. Social networking does not replace going to networking events, meeting people, and exchanging business cards.

Monica: What are some important steps to proper networking?

George: There are three steps in the relationship-building process. I have written about them extensively in my books *Click: Ten Truths for Building Extraordinary Relationships* and *Success Runs In Our Race: The Complete Guide to Effective Networking in the Black Community.*

Identification — The first step is what I call the identification step. This is where you identify people that you want to meet in life. As part of this step, you meet people by circumstance and happenstance. We meet people on elevators, in the mall, on airplanes, and at workshops, seminars, and conferences. The first step is engagement. When we engage a person, we exchange information or niceties. Ultimately, if we like what we feel and see, we exchange business cards or information. That's the first step in the process.

Connecting — The second step in the process is the connecting step. Connecting is based on common ground. Common ground is based on people, places, and things. The more common ground you have with someone, the higher the trust level. The higher the trust, the more willingness a person has to share key concepts and information.

Here's what I know in 30+ years of networking—99.99% of everyone that I've ever given a business card will never, ever follow up. They will never call. They will never reconnect. There are lots of reasons for it, but they won't do it.

Let me give you an example of what I'm talking about. I gave a general session speech at the National Society of Black Engineers in Toronto. This is a wonderful group of 6,000 African Americans in the engineering sciences field. This was two months ago. How many people out of 6,000 do you think have called, e-mailed, or made a connection with me since that time?

Monica: Maybe 10%?

George: No one ever followed up. Were there people in that room that I could help? Probably everyone in that room.

During the 20 minutes that I spoke, I probably changed half the lives there, but no one ever followed up. No one ever said they'd really like to keep in touch and see if there's a way I could help.

The connecting step is the second step in the relationship-building process, but most people fail in that step. This is especially true with African Americans.

Clicking — The third and final step is the clicking step. I wrote an entire book on clicking. Did you ever meet somebody and you just clicked with them? When you click with someone, it simply means that you win, I win, and the people that we serve win. That's the end result of clicking. Most people never get to the clicking step because they never complete the connecting step, which is following up, cultivating, nurturing, and building the relationship.

The other fatal flaw that people make when networking is that they network to get something. Wrong. You network to give. As you give, you get. If you aren't giving, you aren't getting. You cannot take out of life that which you have not put into life, just as you cannot take out of the bank that which you have not put into the bank. That is the first and foremost principle of effective networking. You give first; you share always. The getting comes later.

Monica: You live your life by a set of guiding principles. Would you mind talking about a few of them?

George: Yes. In my book *Click*, I essentially list those principles, and it took me 62 years to write this book because it is the synthesis of the fundamental laws and principles by which I live my life. I'll give you three of them.

The first principle is that you must love, give, serve, and add value. That is the purpose of life. You must live by that purpose and all that is due you will come to you.

The purpose of life is not very complicated because God doesn't make anything complicated. We tend to make things complicated so we don't have to do something and so we can assert control.

Another principle is to bless them and release them. As you grow older and wiser, you must come to the understanding that there are certain people that you must bless and release. You're going to have to rid yourself of toxic people, bloodsuckers, and people who drain you of time, energy, and resources. This is extraordinarily important.

It's easy to say but very difficult to do. Why? Because most of these people are family members, your significant others, or so-called friends. If you're not able to deliver yourself from toxic people and bloodsuckers, you will fail in life. I tell people when you choose your partner, you choose your life. I warn people to not spend major time with minor people. People going nowhere want you to go nowhere with them. People doing nothing want you to do nothing with them. If you want to change your life, change your relationships. It's extraordinarily important.

The third principle is the idea that I trust you first. You must earn my distrust. Now this is completely the opposite of what we are taught. We're taught that people must prove themselves and earn their trust over time. That's not true with me. That's not how I've lived my life. I trust you are who you say you are. I trust that you will deliver what you say you will deliver. I trust that you are an ethical and decent human being. I trust you first and you have to earn distrust.

Now, have I been burned because I trusted the wrong people? Yes. No question about it. The advantages and the wonderful things that have happened and have come to me because I've had that philosophy and attitude in life have far outweighed any disadvantages that I have experienced.

Monica: It is one thing to meet people and to network, but I would imagine that it is important to get them to remember you after you have met. What can people do to make themselves stand out from the crowd?

George: By serving. If you want to be remembered, serve people. Give first. If you want to be forgotten, meet somebody for the first time and start asking for something. If you want to be remembered, meet someone for the first time and say, "I've got something that might be helpful to you," or "I know this person," or "I heard about this job." Give somebody something as fast as you can, such as a compliment. Be the first in the relationship to do that, and you'll be remembered.

Monica: That's wonderful advice. What do you find most rewarding about bringing people together and providing opportunities to learn about the importance of networking and building success?

George: There are literally hundreds of letters and cards I have received from people. They say they have read my book or they heard me say something that absolutely changed their lives. As a result, they have a whole new perspective on life. That is the greatest reward because that's why we're here.

What is Bill Gates doing with his billions of dollars? He's running a foundation and giving away a billion dollars a year. We are here to love, give, serve, and add value. That's how God has designed the system. The more you give, serve, and add value, the more you are paid.

Monica: You have developed a very successful website, Frasernet.com. Can you speak about what people can get from the website and how they can become a member?

George: Our membership is based on a coaching model. We believe that every black person in America needs a coach. If Tiger Woods, Michael Jordan, Lebron James, and the finest executives in Black America have coaches, the average person should also have a coach.

By becoming a member, you will buy into a year-long coaching program. I tell people don't become members of our organization if you don't have goals or objectives for yourself. However, if you have goals, if you want a transformation over the next 12 months, sign up to become a member. We will coach you to achieve that result. When you become a member, you will have access to eight of the top Black coaches in America each month. You will have access to eight of the finest strategists in America.

Monica: You view it from the standpoint that you're investing in your life.

George: That's right. It's your life. It's your results. You're investing in that. I spend about $8,000 to $9,000 per year on personal growth and development conferences, workshops, seminars, books, and CDs. Why? My life is worth it. What is your life worth? Why would you invest $500 or $600 a month in your car but not in yourself? It takes commitment. It takes hard work. It takes tenacity. There are people who, in spite of the fact that they would like to be committed, they are not committed. As my Daddy taught me many years ago, what you do speaks so loudly.

Section 5

Gaining Market Share

Keys to Quickly Gain Market Share

Top business consultant Rebel Brown shares secrets to demystify the fallacy about gaining market share as well as key ideas on how to quickly gain a larger market share in less time.

Rebelizing the Way We Do Business

Rebel Brown—her name says it all. When it comes to business, she is a rebel who has chosen to take the road less traveled, and she's helping her clients obtain amazing results.

Beneath the fiery red hair and bright smile is a tenacious woman who believes in changing the status quo. It's not about how we've always done it—it's about what's happening around you and how you can realign and restructure your business to meet the needs of today's customers.

Defy Gravity is not only the name of her latest book, but it is the basis of her approach to business. If you continue to conduct business "as usual", then you're missing out on many profitable opportunities. As the needs of your customers change, your business approach to fulfilling their needs should evolve as well.

From quickly gaining market share to introducing a new product to changing the way you think about increasing revenue, Rebel shares insights on how entrepreneurs and business owners can improve their business returns by defying gravity in the marketplace. The examples she shares will help you turn your business into a magnet for success.

From "ramp up and roar" to "rescue and restore" to "redefine and rejuvenate," Rebel explains how she uses her leadership skills and tactical strategy to deliver optimum solutions for high-velocity growth. Rebel has worked with over 100 business clients in Europe and the U.S. to help then fund and launch their companies. Now, she's ready to help entrepreneurs channel their energies in new directions. As founder of *Exceptional People Magazine*, I fastened my seatbelt and prepared for liftoff into a new dimension as Rebel began to unleash her approach to defying gravity in the world of business.

Monica: How did you reach the decision that you wanted to help entrepreneurs?

Rebel: I worked for 20 years to gather information. I started out in a corporate environment and I learned from the outside. I had a great mentor early in college tell me that the best way to learn about a business was to start with sales and selling directly to customers. By using this approach, I worked my way into the back office and into marketing and product management.

I started out selling in the computer industry. I sold big systems that were not associated with IBM, which was the most challenging position you could have as your first job. After becoming successful in selling, I moved into marketing jobs. Then I moved into running a product line for a company. That involved a number of considerations.

I began asking, "What is the product?" "What's in the offering?" "How do we market it?" "How do we price it?" "How do we package it?" and "How do we sell it?" It's similar to operating your own business.

The company I worked for was acquired by several international companies. They weren't too happy about having a woman running their top product line. They let me go so they could bring one of their guys in. That's when I started my consulting business.

I started helping small businesses do product planning, marketing launches, and those kinds of things. I focused on helping companies with their product definition. Back then it was start-ups and technology businesses. I helped them find out where their value was, where they could sell, what they could sell, how they could make money, and how to launch into their markets.

I gradually expanded and began working with larger companies. I learned about global markets by operating companies in Europe. The average person has maybe five jobs during their lifetime or has worked for five or six companies. I've worked with over 150 companies.

It was purely exposure to that point. Now, I don't see new problems; I see different circumstances. A lot of our marketing problems are the same.

Even today, people talk about a new economy. New economy problems are similar problems that we've had before because we've had market shifts. It's just that the circumstances of the new economy are different because we've shifted to the industrial age. Then we shifted to more computer usage and automation. Now, we're shifting into an information age where it's a whole different ballgame, even if you're selling products. The dawn of the Internet has changed the way to market, sell, and relate to customers. It's really about being able to look at what's going on in the market, what has shifted, and how to change the way that you look at your business.

You have to interpret the market shifts and take advantage of them versus fearing and trying to avoid them.

Monica: The mentoring that you received was certainly very valuable to you and your business.

Rebel: As I was helping other companies, I learned a broad spectrum of business types and models. I also learned about distributing products and offerings, managing people, and working with various management styles. This allowed me to obtain a broad base of exposure and experience unique problems.

The problems you have in a start-up are very different from the challenges you face in a company that's already grown but has hit a wall. The problems you face in a high-growth company are very different from the problems you face in a company that's crashing and burning. The problems you face in a company whose markets are changing dramatically are very different from those you face with a company where the markets are slower and more sedentary. Having that broad, varying base of exposure helps me assist companies because no two companies are alike.

That's why I wrote *Defy Gravity*. Most strategy books give you a strategy and when you finish them, you say, "Good book, but now what do I do with it?" They also tend to give you one-, two-, or three-step processes. I don't think these processes work because what you need to do for your company may be different from what I need to do. The process may not apply, pure and simple. Two, the strategy books don't tell you what to do. What I wanted to do was write a book to teach people to think differently about their business. If you think differently, you don't need a process. Simply by thinking differently, there will be a shift in your perspective. Then you can start asking questions and you'll view the opportunities differently.

The way to think isn't a one-, two-, or three-step process in a business. Yes, there are certain fundamental rules about business. For example, one of the simple things I teach is we grow our businesses when we deliver distinct value to a market. By following that rule, customers are compelled to buy that value because it solves a problem or it gives them an advantage.

We think we know that basic rule, but then we get stuck in gravity around the very things that keep us from becoming successful. We get stuck in gravity thinking about our value, our markets, and our products. No process is going to change unless you shift the way you're thinking about your business today. Instead of relying on who you were in the past, now you're relying on what your business and your customers need today, and what they will need in the future.

Monica: That's an excellent point.

Rebel: We allow our past to determine our future.

Monica: Quite often we do, yes.

Rebel: That may have worked ten years ago because markets were slower. That doesn't work today. Our success a year ago is not necessarily what's going to make us successful today or in the future. We assume that the same customers will buy for the same reasons. We assume that when we launch a new product, the same people will buy in the same way they did the last time we launched a new product. We pattern things after our past success.

Monica: I guess we take the market for granted.

Rebel: We take it for granted that it hasn't moved. But, in fact, it's moving all over the place.

Monica: I would like to talk about what I'll call your R & R approaches—the ramp-up and roar, the rescue and restore, and the redefine and rejuvenate approaches.

Rebel: Those really aren't approaches. That's just a way to categorize some of the things I do.

Monica: With ramp up and roar, one of the things that you do to help businesses or entrepreneurs is to gain immediate market share in a variety of industries. Is it not true that it usually takes a while to gain market share?

Rebel: That's a fallacy. That's a piece of gravity. I've helped launch over 100 products or companies. One of the places where we have the largest amount of gravity is around how we launch our products or our companies into the market. We tend to do it backwards.

We go out and we develop this product. We keep it secret from our sales force and the market. Then maybe a month before it comes out, we begin to talk about it. A week before it rolls out, we talk to the press. Then we put the press release out and train our sales reps. Now we have this big lightning bolt that says, "Here's our new product," but no one is using it. We have no sales and no revenue. We're starting from that point in time and we have no credibility. That is not the way to become successful in a market launch.

Early on you want to say, "I'm going to take my product concept, go to the top ten target profiles who I think will buy this, and I'm going to test it. Then I'm going to have them begin using it and talking about it quietly."

What you want to do is have customers using your product. You want to have a sales force out selling your product. You want to create a buzz in the market about it before you ever announce it. You want to get what I refer to as *whispering*. You want to get that marketing whisper because everybody wants to know about the thing that only a few people know about.

Monica: I understand what you're speaking about. That sets you up for success.

Rebel: It's also cheaper than the way we usually launch products, it's much more cost effective, and it sets you up to be credible.

Monica: What about your rescue and restore approach?

Rebel: I have a couple of different kinds of things that I do for companies. I differentiate between a turnaround business and a start-around business. A *turnaround business* is the rescue and restore. Last year, I worked with a company that had earned $5 billion in revenue, but they were down to $500 million. That may sound like a lot, but when you've earned $5 billion in the past, that's bad. This is an example of a turnaround because you've got a company that's crippled. As I explain in my flight analogy in *Defy Gravity*, it's like you're spiraling downward and you're getting ready to crash and burn.

The techniques you use in that environment can be different from what you'd use with a start-around business. With a *start-around business*, somebody could say, "OK. I did really well and now I've hit a plateau." "I've hit a wall." "I've stalled and I don't know where to go next." "I need to expand my business." "I need to shift my course." "I need to catch up with my markets." or "I need to find distinct value."

Monica: After reading your book, what can a small business owner take away to help them ramp up their business?

Rebel: I specifically wrote the book so that it could be used by any business owner, whether it's a small business owner or a business executive. The basic fundamentals operate the same, whether I'm a $500 business or a $500 billion business. I wrote the book so that it could be immediately accessible for a small business owner.

The first section discusses gravity and the sources of gravity in businesses. It provides small business owners with a way to look at their businesses and determine how they can attain growth by shifting their perspectives from the way they've always done it. At the end of each section, I have a series of questions and exercises for small business owners, executives, and teams that will help them to identify problems with respect to where they're stuck.

For example, I have a friend who runs a small business called the Oil Region Alliance in Pennsylvania. This business is the equivalent of a chamber of commerce. In this region, they help develop small businesses and invite new businesses to the area. He's got a staff of five people. He's running a nonprofit that is completely funded by other businesses.

He said to me, "I'm a barnacle on everybody's butt. I go out and I am begging for money from businesses that don't have the money. I should be helping them make money instead."

I sent him an advance reader's version of *Defy Gravity* because I wanted his feedback on the book. He called me about a week later and said, "Rebel, I pre-ordered five copies from Amazon. I want to know if I can ship them to you and you can sign them for my team."

I said, "Sure, but why? Randy, what got you so excited?"

He said, "Rebel, you just solved the problem I've had for a year. I've been so focused on the struggle of how I provide enough value so that these people will donate to me."

He shared about what happened when he did one of the exercises in the book. He said, "I went through the book and I did the following exercise: *List the things you know to be true about your business*. I wrote down the following items: I help develop businesses in the local geography. I have a team of five people who have over 80 years of combined business development expertise. I am funded by donations from other businesses."

And then he says, "That's when it hit me. Who says I have to be funded by donations?"

He continued, "My two top guys and I have been through three economic ups and downs and have helped businesses grow through those times. So I said to myself, 'Why don't I go out and sell myself and my executives as consultants to the businesses that need our help?' Instead of going out and asking for donations, I will go out and offer consulting services. I will help them find ways to grow their business. They will pay me and the revenues will fund my nonprofit."

He was stuck in the gravity of one word—*donations*. All he did was change donations to revenue and his entire business model changed. Why was he stuck on that?

Because traditionally nonprofits are funded by donations. Says who? This is an example of the way we've always thought about it or done it. In this new economy, you have to shift your perspective from that kind of gravity to growth-oriented thinking.

We are natural-born gravity creators because it's in our DNA. We create it. It's the only reason it exists. We learn from our experiences, both positive and negative. We learn from other people. As kids, we learn from our parents, siblings, playmates, and teachers. In business, we learn from our experiences and our mentors. We also learn from what we hear and what we know. As we learn, we create beliefs about ourselves, our world, and our business. Over time those beliefs become more formalized until they become facts and knowns.

Monica: Yes, absolutely

Rebel: Over time, those facts and knowns become tradition, status quo, and the way we've always done it.

Monica: And traditions become hard to break.

Rebel: They become gravity. All of a sudden, you'll find that because we learned from these experiences, we create gravity. The experience we had a year ago doesn't necessarily apply to what's real today because the markets around us are changing so quickly. We get stuck into this status quo belief of, "Well, that's the way we've always done it. We've always served customers that way. That's what they love about our value."

Maybe that was true last year, but guess what? It doesn't matter today. It changed. That customer changed. What's available to them has changed. Look at the Internet. Would you have thought five years ago that the Internet would become the major delivery system for information, products, and e-commerce?

People didn't see that coming. Would you have thought five years ago that Facebook and Twitter would be a way for you to interact and build customer relationships? Even a year ago you may not have thought that, but if you're not doing it today, you're behind. You have to constantly make those shifts.

Monica: You have to think not only outside the box, but well beyond it. As a matter of fact, you shouldn't think of yourself as being in a box.

Rebel: You have to think well beyond the box that you've always been in. I don't care what kind of small business you're in today. The way you ran your business five years ago, two years ago, or even a year ago is not going to be successful for you in the future.

Monica: That is true. You take small steps first.

Rebel: It's shifting from the "Nobody wins in this economy, and I can't grow." to "In any economy there are opportunities, and the question is, where is mine?" I need to shift my thinking to find it, and I will find it.

A lot of this is human behavior. You can't separate human behavior from business behavior. The other thing that happens is if you look around us, we are bombarded with negativity, such as people saying, "Nobody succeeds in this economy." or "Business is bad." There are successes everywhere. The news doesn't cover them because success doesn't sell.

There are successful businesses all over this market, both small and large. When we get bombarded by negativity, our natural human instinct is to hunker down into the way we've always done it and into what we know is safe and comfortable.

Monica: That is true. Sometimes people want to feel comfortable with situations that are uncomfortable. They become comfortable because they're afraid to move forward.

Rebel: Right, because it's known.

Keys to Quickly Gain Market Share

Leading online office supply icon Tony Ellison shares key points on differentiating your business from your biggest competitors and thus increasing your market share.

A Unique Value Proposition Equals Success

You might say that Tony Ellison has changed the way business owners shop for office supplies and many other products. You may recall the early years when the Internet first began to show some signs of longevity. Who would have thought that it would become the gold mine that it is today? In 1994, Tony Ellison realized how beneficial the Internet would be for retailers.

As the founder and CEO of Shoplet.com, Ellison's vision to change the way business owners and corporate America shop for business products has revolutionized the office products industry. While working as a senior executive for Goldman Sachs' technology division, Ellison's foresight into the Internet's capability led him to start his company, which today offers stiff competition for brick-and-mortar retailers.

One might say that it takes courage to go against the "big boys" in the brick-and-mortar arena like OfficeMax, Staples, and Office Depot. As an e-tailer, Shoplet.com has become an extraordinary success every quarter since Ellison guided the company to profitability in 1997.

Ellison's tremendous success didn't come from "doing business as usual." He defied the status quo. He took an innovative approach to the customer's shopping experience by developing proprietary e-procurement software and platforms, boosting selection and distribution, and including a wide array of environment-friendly products. The website has also been optimized to serve mobile customers who now have the ability to place orders without having to use a computer.

These unique approaches have enabled him to rise above the competition each year. Shoplet.com is now No. 142 on a list of

Top 500 Online Retailers. Ellison enthusiastically shared with *Exceptional People Magazine* his story and the impact that his business has made on the lives of entrepreneurs, their customers, and his customers.

Monica: You have built an amazing online business that seems to be surpassing many of your competitors. Your company, Shoplet.com, is known as an e-tailer. You sell and distribute products strictly online. Can you describe the types of products that you offer?

Tony: We were founded in 1994 with the very simple vision—to carry the widest and largest selection of office, business, break room, and industrial products. We've been true to that promise. Today, we carry over 400,000 products in categories such as traditional office supplies, IT, furniture, janitorial supplies, industrial, furniture, technology, and much more. Our products are even shipped for free on most orders over $45.

We cover quite a few categories and a very large spectrum. This is one of the key differentiating factors between Shoplet and the big boys, such as Staples, Office Depot, and Office Max. While we have over 400,000 products, an average superstore only carries 6,000 items. The biggest one that I've seen in the country has no more than 10,000. So we have almost 40 times more products than our competitors.

Monica: You have experienced steady growth every quarter since about 1997. How are you able to continuously increase revenue as an e-tailer versus what the brick-and-mortar stores are doing?

Tony: It's worth noting that we are currently ranked as the number one virtual e-tailer in our category. We have also successfully subscribed over 2.8 million customers. Going forward, that gives us enormous scale.

When we got into this office supply arena, it was already crowded by four large players who dominated the space. We needed to come up with a unique value proposition based on service, simplicity, and selection that would help us to sustain a competitive advantage in the marketplace. For us, the first thing was selection.

We were looking at differentiating ourselves in the marketplace so that we could have an edge. If you remember back in 1994, the Internet was just forming. The big boys were very slow to move. The industry that we are in is the second-largest traded industry online after travel. I saw that as a great opportunity to have a first-mover advantage.

What was really interesting as we were building our web presence was the fact that the big boys were using the web as a means to take orders online and reduce the transaction cost. That's one of the key differentiators. In addition to receiving online orders, we also sought to have a niche market with green products. We have the largest green and environment-friendly products online. We've done so many other great things to encourage the transition to eco-friendly products.

Additionally, we have started understanding the small- and medium-sized business customer. These businesses can be a 25-person company or a 2,000-person company. They wanted to get the same benefits that Fortune 500 companies were enjoying when they were transacting. Many of them wanted to have access to a costly e-procurement management application called Ariba. The starting cost is $750,000.

I don't know many small businesses that can afford that kind of pricing for streamline their purchasing process. We took the best features of Ariba, implemented them for free, and hosted our own e-procurement platform. We are now forwarding it to all of our customers.

Another requirement we found with our small- and medium-sized customers is that they wanted to get the same volume discounts that the Fortune 500 companies were enjoying. We went back to the suppliers, negotiated favorably, and we passed all the discounts to our small- and medium-sized customers. That really helped us to differentiate ourselves.

Many online players would build what is called a transactional site. Shoplet is all about building a relational site, which means we're all about repeat and retention. We want the customer to come back to us. We took a lesson from Amazon's chapter and we built a phenomenal online customer experience. I'm not saying we are perfect, but we strive very hard to meet and exceed our customers' expectations every day.

Service is a really key differentiator for us as well. While our competitors, like Office Depot, have sought to outsource their customer service to third-world countries to reduce cost, we have kept our customer service in-house. We felt that this was the most important element of what we have to offer as a differentiator to our customers. That strategy has worked flawlessly for us.

Monica: Through your thought process you have come up with ways in which to not only grow your business quickly and successfully, but you have outmaneuvered the brick-and-mortar stores.

Tony: Absolutely. When you talk about our growth, it has been exceptional. For the past decade, we've been growing both in down and up economies and in one of the worst economies, too. For example, from 2001 to 2006, we grew in triple digits each year. If you remember, back then it was both a down and up economy. In the last four or five years, in one of the worst economies we've seen in our lifetime, we still managed to achieve strong, aggressive, double-digit growth.

In 2009, many companies had either gone out of business or had experienced sales declines and layoffs. We have not only increased our head count by more than 45 percent, our sales grew in excess of 40 percent. We are definitely bucking the trend. The value proposition we put in front of the customer is widely and favorably received.

Monica: How are you passing along the savings and discounts from the manufacturers or vendors and still making money? How are you able to continue to increase revenue?

Tony: That's a good question. When you look at this industry, it's an old industry that has seen very little change in the past 100 years. When you look at the cost of retail, and sustain that kind of operation, it's overwhelming as opposed to having an online outfit that is a lot slimmer, leaner, and meaner in that sense. Our cost is vastly different from the "big boys." Retail has become a liability in this industry, and in order for them to pay for that type of expense, they have to build that into the price.

There is a substantial discount between what we offer our customers versus what they are offering. On a daily basis, when we go to customers with an average staff size of 250 people, we save them anywhere between 15-30 percent. That's enormous when you consider that an average person buys $500 worth of office supplies in a year. That's almost $45K a year in quantifiable savings.

Monica: What gave you the idea of starting a company like Shoplet versus some other type of Internet business where you don't have to be concerned with so many products?

Tony: Before starting Shoplet, I was working at Goldman Sachs on Wall Street. In 1994, when the Internet was forming, I understood that the Internet, and e-commerce specifically, was going to level the playing field. This was going to allow small businesses to compete effectively with large businesses. The Internet was also going to become more efficient for small- and medium-sized businesses to transact. That was one key.

What really attracted me to the office product industry was the fact that it was a large industry. Those products did not need to be touched before being ordered. For instance, if you ordered paper and knew the brand, you also ordered pencils and notebooks. Therefore, you're more likely to order that product online without needing to go to the store and touch it. That was one of the key reasons we decided to jump into it.

The online market was very fragmented and underserved. When we combined those reasons, we felt that they were strong and compelling reasons to jump into it. When I was thinking of leaving my job, people thought that I was losing it. I had to give up a very stable salary and a very comfortable environment. I'm thankful to my wife for being so supportive. She said, "If this is really your vision and your dream, you should go for it and live a life of no regrets."

Monica: What are your views on the Internet as a whole in terms of all of its current capabilities? Where do you think it's headed?

Tony: It's interesting. I think about it every day. We've seen such a rapid change online. If you look at the last 10 years, Google came on the scene and has changed the economy as we know it. Now we have an even stronger and bigger force coming with social networking.

Facebook is social-driven recommendation and a whole lot more powerful. Those are some of the big trends. We see social commerce developing more rapidly than we've ever seen before. I think with HTML5 developing, new specs emerging, and online development platforms becoming more powerful, we're going to see more features. Let's not forget Twitter and some of the other new technologies.

Monica: Can you share a couple of things about how your life has changed as a business owner versus working as a senior executive for Goldman Sachs?

Tony: I want to set proper expectations for all entrepreneurs. I never expected it to be as difficult, especially in the first three years. It's non-stop, around-the-clock work. It's those critical years from formation to establishing yourself to putting a footprint in the ground.

How has it transformed my lifestyle? Vastly! It's to the point where in the first three years I was probably working 10 times harder than I was doing before. Maybe I'm exaggerating just a little because I was working hard already.

It wasn't a walk in the park. I never said, "Hey I'm my own boss and I'm going to design my own hours." It's never been like this for me. It's constant, around-the-clock thinking about your go-to-market strategies and your business model. In one sense it gave me an enormous amount of freedom. At the same time, I was so preoccupied with this idea that it engulfed me.

Monica: Of course, at the same time, you had already established a very good financial foundation where you could branch out on your own.

Tony: That's absolutely true. That's probably what made it happen for me. That has been a blessing in disguise for us. One of the things it did is allowed us to be independent. We don't dance on anybody else's whims. We make decisions based on whatever is good for business rather than investors. The customer really is the center stage for us. That has been a huge, liberating factor for Shoplet. I could tell you now, after 17 years, that I have more artistic freedom. I'm more at liberty to make decisions on my own and be in control of my destiny.

Monica: Many people want to be in control of their future and they are asking, "How can I do that?" You have to start at the bottom and work your way up. There's just no getting around that.

Tony: Absolutely not.

Monica: For the new entrepreneur or the person that wants to become an entrepreneur, can you offer some important tips to help them grow their business, whether it's an online or offline business?

Tony: First of all, don't be afraid to make mistakes. I'm sure I've made countless mistakes. There is no such thing as starting a business and doing everything right. Making mistakes is part of the learning process. Second, when you have an idea, make sure that it's an idea that is sustainable and gives you a competitive advantage in the marketplace. Make sure when you're starting up that you have a business model that includes a unique value proposition to your customer and understand why that would make you successful. Most importantly, try to study your marketplace beforehand. Understand that void and try to address that rather than copying somebody else's idea.

If we just tried to become another Staples or Office Depot, we wouldn't be as successful. We sought to innovate, offer many green products, and are eco-friendly in terms of what we have to offer to the future generation, and that's what makes us successful. When you look at the green movement, it's real and every single person has an obligation to leave the planet as good as they found it.

Monica: I want to talk about customer loyalty because I think sometimes business owners don't realize the importance of keeping a good customer. They are so excited to get a customer, but then they don't really have anything in place to turn them into loyal customers. Can you talk about how a business owner can turn that customer into a loyal customer?

Tony: One thing that helped us to stay above waters in the worst times is our ability to concentrate on repeat customers. We have extensive retention strategies, which start with understanding the customer's lifetime value and being able to say, "This is really what the customer is worth." The customer's experience is crucial. You need to be able to target them, mine their data, know who the niche customers are, and know the customers that you want to come back. We have a 110% price match guarantee to please our customers.

Try to build a loyalty program such as a reward initiative or data-driven marketing campaigns. These campaigns can be done through e-mails, at the point of purchase, or in general marketing campaigns that will bring the customers back. You cannot start a business without having a repeat and retention strategy that is data driven.

Monica: It's much easier to get a repeat customer than it is to get a new customer.

Tony: That's absolutely right. At the end of the day, when you are building a company, it's about people. You need to build a team of excellent people.

Section 6

Employees and Management

Keys to Attract the Right Employees

Human resource expert and consultant Cori Maedel, CEO of Jouta, Inc., shares key elements in selecting the right people to help you meet your business goals.

Organizational Clarity: Effectively Manage Your Business

With over 25 years of experience in the human resources and business development arenas, Cori Maedel is armed with the knowledge needed to help small businesses and corporations overcome obstacles in dealing with employment issues.

As founder and CEO of the Jouta Performance Group, she has enabled businesses to figure out the best approach to their human resource requirements. She helps business owners avoid costly mistakes. Her company offers many personal and professional consulting services to help businesses create an infrastructure that will attract and retain quality employees.

Maedel provides practical advice for small business owners and suggests policies to implement for recruiting, development, retention, and training. She's always ready to answer questions from business owners related to building effective and successful teams. In her interview with *Exceptional People Magazine*, Maedel shared her success working with clients.

Monica: Can you talk about how you became involved in human resources (HR)?

Cori: When I was younger, HR was really a policing sort of place. They were the people that hired and fired you. Twenty-five years ago, HR really wasn't a place that I was interested in at all. But I was fortunate enough to work in an organization that was doing some innovative things outside of the HR umbrella. Early on, we were doing total-quality management where we were taking an organization that had been around for 40 years and putting a team environment in place.

I found that I had an ability to work with people. Somehow, they trusted me. I was able to empathize with them. So, I had a combination of connecting with people and the ability to do HR work. I was also a born entrepreneur. My parents are both entrepreneurs, and I had an incredibly strong work ethic that I learned from my mother. I was constantly looking around and thinking, "What can I do differently here? How can I improve?" I was always looking at ways to do things better.

Monica: How has being in business for yourself changed your life?

Cori: I've wanted to start my own company for as long as I can remember, but couldn't decide what I wanted to do. The thing that surprised me the most is how much I would be up against myself. One of the things I committed to is that I would walk my talk. I work with so many executive teams, so any advice I gave them I had to follow. If I was OK to preach to them, then I better walk my talk. Any time I came into a crossroads at Jouta, I would look back at what advice I had given and made sure I took my own advice.

It has been an amazing process to come up against my own beliefs and understandings and to constantly learn how to be better, get more balance, and do everything that you have to do as an entrepreneur well.

Monica: What do you find most rewarding about helping other business owners build effective teams and bring on the best employees?

Cori: In my early teens, I was a pretty troubled kid. I was making bad choices, and there was nobody in my environment that could help me. My mom didn't have the skill. After that, I decided that I would do everything I could to help people. That was the start.

As I was helping people and organizations and bringing them together, the reward was amazing. For me to see an organization turn one degree and do things better, there's nothing better than that. I believe that I come from a place of giving now. I switched to that perspective throughout my life. Now it's about how I can make a difference in the lives of the people that I touch, for both organizations and individuals alike. Each organization is nothing more than a whole bunch of people.

So many entrepreneurs go out there and they have these amazing businesses, but they are only masters of their own craft. There is so much that they don't know. Normally, they come to us at the time a pain point. These turning points could be terminating an employee or needing more structure for rapid growth. It's so great to be able to say, "I know I can make a difference here." I know I can make a difference for that entrepreneur. I know I can help them sleep better at night because I can take care of some of the things that I know are bothering them.

Monica: Is there a good or a bad time to hire employees? As a new business owner, when is the best time to hire employees?

Cori: When you're a brand-new business, and you've got a million things that you're doing, you have to realize when you've got too much. One of the things I say when I work with small business owners is, "Make a list of all the things that you have to do in a day." I'm talking about everything from cleaning the floors to the IT work to the sales and marketing. Then I ask them to categorize their tasks. Once they categorize them, I get them to look at it. Next, I ask, "What can you do here?" and "What do you need help with?" I help them identify what they can do, what they need help with, and we build it from there.

I think the ideal time to hire new employees is at the point where you think, "OK. I've done all that I can do. Now I need help to take myself to the next level." If entrepreneurs take themselves down the road to where they actually burn themselves out and can't sustain the level of intensity they need, then they're not going to be successful.

I think there are different types of entrepreneurs. There are ones that really want to start companies and those that want to take contracts here and there and manage on their own.

Monica: From a business owner's perspective, how can one attract the right candidates for the job?

Cori: That's a great question. Traditionally, at the start I'll see organizations or entrepreneurs focus on nothing but sales. In those instances, I see lots of businesses fail. You need to set up an infrastructure. You need to have a place where, if you're going to hire an employee, they're going to know you have your act together. That means ensuring that you're not grabbing the first employee that you find, being clear on what you're looking for, and understanding what you need and where you're going as a company.

I remember when I moved to our first office, the first thing that I did was make sure that the place was set up so when we hired an employee that person would enjoy being there. This may sound crazy, but I made sure that the kitchen was stocked with knives, forks, plates, cups, and dishes. I made sure that the office was comfortable and productive so that when the employee came in, the response would be, "Wow! I can work here."

I think we've grown organically and pretty solidly because of the way that I handled it. I made sure there was structure in place. I understood the people component so that when I brought people in, I took care of the organization. I also made sure I had the right employment agreement. Another thing I did with my very first employee was to offer benefits. Could I afford that? Not really.

Monica: Most small business owners can't.

Cori: I couldn't either, but I knew if I was going to attract the right people to help me as I grew, I had to be able to invest in them. There are different ways you can go about doing it. In Canada, there are ways to invest in people that are probably a bit easier than in the United States, but it's possible. The problem is entrepreneurs don't get help to find out what is possible. They go on what they know to be true around the service or the offering.

It's amazing to me the amount of times that I have walked into companies and I asked employees what their biggest challenge was. One of the biggest drains on productivity is the fact that there isn't a structure in place. There isn't consistent treatment and behavior of employees.

Because they don't have a lot of money, entrepreneurs often feel that they have to compromise. When they compromise, they may often promise things that they can't deliver. They'll say things like, "When we get really big, I'm going to give you 10 percent of the company." They don't think about five years from now. They think about right now. That's where entrepreneurs get in trouble. I'm always thinking five years out because whatever I'm doing, it has to be sustainable and it has to grow with us.

When I put a practice in place, I know what it's going to look like five years down the road. Entrepreneurs are often challenged when they're just starting their company. Many of them don't have a business background. I'll say, "You're working on hiring your first person. What are some of the things you want to establish as practices for your employees going forward?"

The problem is they don't know what they want right now. I could say to them, "Here are some policies you should put in place. Maybe you should have a sick leave policy." We have a policy that we recommend called the *patio pass*. On long weekends during the summer, the staff gets to utilize one patio pass and leave early on a Friday.

There are different variations of that offer. The problem is entrepreneurs don't know the business well enough and don't know their staff's tolerance level well enough. For example, one company was implementing a sick leave policy that stated that employees weren't eligible to have any sick time until they had worked for the company for three months. What we implemented instead was a policy that stated that the minute you started working with us, you got sick time. So when the very first employee needed to take sick time within the first three months, which is a probationary period in Canada, the client flipped out.

He said, "Oh my, this person has only worked for me for a month and he is taking sick time."

I said, "Yes, I know. But this is what we decided."

He said, "I don't like that."

So sometimes entrepreneurs don't know what their tolerance levels are.

Monica: How can they recover from that?

Cori: We recommend to employers that if you're putting policies in an employee handbook, commit to making changes only once a year. Often what happens is that employers put things in their handbooks, but they are also constantly changing them because of something that's happened. It's a reactive and emotional response.

I said to my client, "Our practice is to only change the employee handbook once a year. In the fall of that year we review it. Do you still want to change this?"

He said, "Yes."

Then we knew that there were no employees currently working that would be affected because everybody had already passed probation. It was an easy practice to change. The new handbook for 2010 said that you had to pass probation before you could take sick time. So you can change some rules. You just have to do it in a way that is compliant with the law. Also, if you're changing anything fundamentally, you have to make sure you balance that.

Entrepreneurs don't know what they don't know. At Jouta, we have well over 90 years of experience in these things. You know the great thing for us? If there is a question to be asked, chances are we've been asked that question.

Monica: How important are job descriptions?

Cori: I think what's important before you start hiring people is to absolutely know what you need that person to do. I think where people get into trouble with job descriptions is they create a job description, hire someone based on it, and then ignore it all together. It's a piece of paper that gets put away.

You first have to get really clear about what you need. What's the profile? What skills do you need? What are the knowledge, skills, and ability you need?

I like saying that you need to create a job profile because every time an employee comes in, they're never going to do everything that's on there. Again, it depends on how detailed it is. It depends on the ability someone to craft that information.

Entrepreneurs have trouble being clear on what they want the person to do. The clearer they can be up front, the better. I think job profiles are critically important. In order for that profile to be effective in the long term, it needs to be maintained. Far too often they're not.

Another piece that gets entrepreneurs in trouble is that they build recruitment based on the individual versus what the company needs. For instance, they hire the first person and take whatever skills that person brings. Hopefully, they've done a detailed job description. Then that person comes in and starts doing other things. So, when that person leaves, the entrepreneur will say, "Oh, I've got to fill that person's position."

I say to them, "Wait a second. The role is the important factor, not what that person did. What should that role be and are they the same?" I find that often they're not the same because entrepreneurs don't step back and do the planning around the positions they need for their organizations.

They don't ask themselves, "What duties should be performed," "Are all the right people in the right places?" and "Who do I need to hire to fulfill those requirements?"

Monica: Otherwise you're not getting the best out of them.

Cori: You're absolutely right.

Monica: From an entrepreneurial standpoint, what can employers do to reduce the turnover rate in an up economy, and if the economy is down, how can they keep the employees satisfied and give them incentives?

Cori: I think this all comes down to one word—*clarity*. You need organizational clarity. The entrepreneur has to be really clear about who the company is and make sure that everybody working for him or her knows exactly what the company stands for. They need to be held accountable to objectives that help drive the business.

So many companies as they start to grow don't stop and say, "We need to make sure everybody's on the same page. We need to make sure everybody knows exactly where we're going so we're all headed in the same direction." It's easy to motivate people when times are good.

When times are tough, it can be an empowering experience for employees because they can rally around you and help you grow. They can help you through the tough time.

But if they don't know what's going on, how could they possibly do that? When we work with companies, one of the main things we do is make sure that everything is integrated so there is clarity. If I go into a company and I ask the same 10 questions of 10 employees, I may get 10 different answers. They may not be 100% different, but I could get a majority of responses that are. If that's the case, not only am I not motivated because I'm not clear on what I'm doing, I'm not clear on the impact I'm having with this company.

It's all about organizational clarity. People talk about mission and vision. Those are overused words. At the same point, they're critical. We have a purpose to make sure any client we touch is in a better position than they were before we got there.

Entrepreneurs often don't do that. They don't make sure everybody knows. They often say, "People know."

I counter and say, "They don't know."

If you're not talking to them, not sharing with them, and not telling them where they're going and what they're doing, they are going to lose sight of the vision and their connection to it. If I'm clear about the role I play, I know where we're going as a company, and I know when times are tough or good, I'm going to rally when things are down.

Monica: How do you measure the success of your company?

Cori: A big way we measure our success is by repeat customers, long-term clients, and referrals. Most of our business is referral based. You can measure it by revenue, but that's easy. It's all about our reputation in the industry. What's our reputation within our company and with our clients? How do our employees feel about us? For me, it's also honoring all that we say is important to us. It's something we live by on a consistent basis. If we're doing all of those things, then I know the rest will come.

That's the foundation. Somebody said to me the other day, "What's your financial goal?" I said, "We've got financial goals because that's something we have to measure." We need budgets and all that. But for me it's about our growing organically—not too fast for the sake of the money. It's about growing in a way that we can manage as an organization. I think many companies get the sale and then they figure out how to service it. We know how to service it and then we get the sale. When we go in and say, "This is what we can do," we actually can. I've seen too many companies go, "OK, now what? Everybody scramble."

Monica: I've often heard people say, "Go ahead and say yes. Then you can figure out how to do it."

Cori: I think that's the constant approach within organizations. That approach must be working because many of them do it. But my question is "At what cost?" What's the cost to the employees? What's the cost to the bottom line? That approach is going to create incredible amounts of inefficiency and messy productivity. If you've got to call people in and you've got an 11th hour fire to put out, that approach is not as efficient as having a system in place.

Monica: Do you focus on issues such as workplace violence and bullying with your clients?

Cori: Yes. One of my clients, who had been told to contact us for over a year, hadn't done so because the individual thought they were fine. I received three bullying complaints against one employee and a sexual harassment letter against another. That's a tough thing because it's about the leadership. How did it get to a point where that kind of behavior was OK? I'm not saying that it was OK, but not knowing about it is not an OK answer.

If that was my organization, I would take 100% responsibility. If I saw it or somebody knew it was happening, it would get stopped immediately. But when you don't have those practices in place and you don't have the kind of leaders in place who understand how to deal with those situations, things like that are going to happen.

This particular leader, who is a lovely individual, just said, "I didn't know it was going on."

I said, "How didn't you know?"

The behavior was literally happening within ten feet of him. I know he knew, but he kept hoping it would go away.

What they underestimate is that when they ignore it, it festers and productivity suffers. One of the things I do with the team is I sit down with each employee. We go for lunch and we talk about expectations. We talk about what I expect of them and what they expect of me to make sure that we understand where everyone is coming from. One of the things I say to them is, "If you ever have an issue with me about anything, you don't come to me when it's happening, and you take it home and you fester with it, shame on you." I want to set up an environment that no matter what it is, we can talk about it.

One of the things I say to people is to never have a conversation with someone who isn't present. You have to set up a culture that's safe to do that. They need to know that it doesn't matter what it is, we've got to be able to be open and communicative with each other. That becomes more difficult the bigger you get.

Monica: I've worked in many environments over the years where employees have had issues with their manager or management. What kind of personality or characteristics should an effective manager have?

Cori: That's a loaded question. There's a difference between managing and leading. A manager is going to be someone who is really strong on the tactical side of things and is going to help get the day-to-day stuff done. They need to know their craft. They need to know the rules. A manager also has to have a leadership component. With leadership, the most important thing is consistency. You have to treat people consistently. There are days when it's hard for me and the stress is over my head. Even during those times, I still work really hard to come in here and my employees will not know a thing. We change as human beings when we're in stressful situations.

We have to be consistent, fair, and open. Employees have to know what you expect of them. You have to have open communication with your staff. I meet with each individual on my team. I talk to them about the type of culture that we have and the expectations we have concerning communication. I had someone come work for us who didn't like the idea that we didn't talk behind each other's back.

She was only with us for a month because she started doing it. Right away, I took a look and said, "This is inherently who she is. She won't fit here." When you're a good manager and a leader, you make tough decisions quickly. We go to companies where an employee has been there 20 years. They should have left 20 years ago but nobody did anything about it. They just think, "OK, we'll get by." But that starts severing your culture. I'm not willing to compromise our values.

Monica: One of the things that you focus on is what you refer to as bridging the gap between business and people. Can you talk a little bit about that?

Cori: Bridging of the gap occurs when the entrepreneur and the employees are completely in sync. When clarity exists, I can walk over that bridge, walk over to you as my employer, know I'm going to be treated fairly, and know that everything that I'm doing counts. I understand how it's being measured. I can stand tall at the end of the day and say, "Wow! I did some great work."

The organization can walk to the entrepreneur and walk over the bridge to the employee and say, "Wow! Who is that motivated, productive employee? We're a team. We're cohesive."

Monica: What advice can you give the small business owner or entrepreneur to get them excited about finding the right approach to expand their business in terms of employees or management?

Cori: If I had the perfect answer to that, I'd be a kajillionaire. Here's what I can tell you. I preached to entrepreneurs, big companies, and everybody in between for 20+ years. I told them all the things that they needed to do. Then I said, "I'm going to put my money where my mouth is. I'm going to walk my talk. I'm going to start my own company."

Not only did I walk my talk and do everything I ever preached about, I absolutely know with certainty the difference it makes. I'm not sitting here preaching and going, "I don't know if this really works or not. I know it works."

I think entrepreneurs have to understand what they're good at—and that there are areas that they don't know. If they just did that assessment early on and said, "I'm a killer salesperson but this people stuff, I have no idea," or "I'm a killer people person and I need sales help." Wherever their strengths are, they have to align themselves with individuals who can support them in those areas. There are lots of creative ways to do that. One of the reasons we started this company was because many companies aren't at a stage where a full-time person makes sense. It makes more sense to have us on a part-time basis.

I am honestly not so good at accounting. The first thing I made sure I had was an accountant. I knew that that was an area where I was not going to excel. I don't know how to help people understand that absolutely everything is built on the people you hire. You can take any road you want, but if you want the easy road, you have to put practices in place. Really be clear about what you want. Do some R&D up front. Many companies just get started on the corner of a napkin at a meeting.

I spent a lot of time really thinking about what I wanted this company to become and then built it. I haven't deviated very much. The only instances when I've deviated are when the market dictated that I needed to deviate. Other than that, my goal and my vision remain completely intact.

Creative Staff Perks for Small Business Owners

Employee benefits are usually considered to be the basic employer-provided benefits, such as health insurance, paid vacation and sick time, and a retirement plan. Perks are all of the other fringe benefits that are included in an overall benefits package. They give small business owners an opportunity to attract and retain top talent without spending a lot of money.

As a small business owner, you often can't offer expensive perks to your employees, but you still need to compete for great talent just like the larger corporations. The competition for top employees is causing compensation costs to rise tremendously, and small business owners must find a way to get a piece of the talent pie. As a result, smaller businesses need to be more creative to produce perks and benefits to motivate and keep great employees.

Perks are usually not considered part of the normal compensation plan. They are considered positive rewards for a job well done, a tool that can be used to retain employees, and incentives that can create a positive working environment.

When developing a rewards system, you may consider creating some perks that can be applied across the board. You may also single out specific individuals who have done an excellent job. With a small amount of imagination and creativity, you can develop low-cost perks that will amaze your employees and build loyalty. Creating perks to help attract and retain top talent should be considered a high priority for small business owners.

Here are some ideas to consider when creating employee perks:

- Sponsor a company-wide picnic or lunch at a local restaurant to keep all of your employees motivated.

- For employees who put in extra hours, complete urgent projects, or go the extra mile, treat them to lunch or give them a gift certificate to their favorite store.

- Offer a movie voucher or tickets as a small gesture of appreciation for providing excellent customer service. You can also give them away spontaneously to employees who go beyond the call of duty.

- Give employees a half or full day off to show appreciation. However, you should use caution when implementing this type of perk because it can harm productivity over time.

- If everyone does not have to be in the office within a specific time frame, you can offer flex time. This is a great way to show them that you care about their personal lives and obligations outside the workplace. You may also consider telecommuting for employees who have to travel long distances to and from work.

- Give employees small cash rewards. Never underestimate the power of cash.

- Give restaurant gift cards.

- Contribute to the continuing education of your employees. Determine the dollar amount that you can afford to give each employee and encourage them to use it to enhance their skills.

- Sponsor an afternoon ice cream or pizza social.

- Give them an afternoon off to play putt-putt golf.

- Offer employee memberships in professional or trade associations. Often, employees want to network with peers in their field and broaden their horizons. It's an excellent opportunity for them to learn new ideas, gain additional knowledge, and implement them in your company.

- Present a certificate of appreciation to employees who have achieved a high level of productivity or completed a special project much earlier than expected. Certificates can be announced and presented during a staff meeting.

Recruiting top talent can be a challenge, but once you hire them, it will be to your advantage to find creative ways to keep them. Keeping your existing employees long-term will reduce turnover rates and reduce the time and costs associated with hiring, screening, interviewing, and training new employees. Reducing high turnover rates also increases employee morale.

Losing seasoned employees with great experience, expertise, and knowledge of your company and business processes can be costly. They thoroughly understand your customers' needs. New employees may not be able to deliver the same level of high-quality service early on, and your customers want to receive quality services and products consistently. If you are continually bringing on new employees, it may result in lost customers.

Your employees are a significant investment. Make sure you develop a package that will keep them motivated to stay. If presented the right way, smaller rewards often work just as well as expensive rewards. If you show that you care about them, they will thank you by remaining loyal and continue providing quality work.

Section 7

Negotiating: How to Get What You Want

8 Secrets to Effectively Negotiate Anything

Expert negotiator Greg Williams shares secrets on how to perfect your negotiating skills to get what you want.

A Candid Conversation with the Master Negotiator

Greg Williams has been dubbed The Master Negotiator. His understanding of how to "work a deal" has made him sought after by major corporations, politicians, and others. There's more to negotiating than meets the eye. Williams has tremendous insights to offer anyone who wants to perfect their negotiation skills.

As a consultant to Fortune 500 corporations, Williams has provided award-winning consulting services to clients such as Dun & Bradstreet, Bank of America, Home Depot, the Xerox Corporation, and many others.

His mother taught him many lessons about negotiating. She instilled in him the value of money and how to make it last by negotiating for everything. He's negotiated multi-million-dollar deals on behalf of clients and has trained many people to become savvy negotiators. His list of achievements is a testament to his ability to conduct successful negotiations.

Williams is the bestselling author of *Negotiate: Afraid, 'Know' More—How to Negotiate Your Way to Success*. He is an exceptional businessman, an inspiring keynote speaker, and a seminar leader who candidly shares in-depth insights into achieving successful negotiations.

Monica: As a child, how did you know you had the skill and talent to become a negotiator?

Greg: As a kid growing up, I had the opportunity to see my mother and grandmother negotiate for everything. We were poor, and we had to make our dollars stretch. At times I would become somewhat embarrassed by the fact they'd ask for discounts or ask for more than what was offered.

When I was about seven or eight years old, my mother said to me one time, "Look, it's your money. Why do you get embarrassed? Wouldn't you rather keep more of your money than give it to someone else?"

That was when the idea first struck me—if you know how to negotiate you can get more of what you're seeking. I began implementing some of the tactics and strategies that I saw my mother and grandmother use. I thought, "This is fascinating how people not only react to you, but also how much you can receive as a result of asking for things." You can achieve much as a result of people being appreciative that you gave them the recognition they deserved.

Basically, that is what negotiations are all about. I tell people you're always negotiating because any aspect of life that you're engaged in, you're exchanging information. That was something else that I found out as I began my career. As a result of information that I had about a particular client or target, I was able to understand them when they conveyed a certain sentiment to me. At the same time, I understood what they needed and I met their needs in order to get what I wanted.

Monica: Was there a specific lesson your mother taught you that laid the foundation for you to become an expert negotiator?

Greg: When I was about 16 or 17 years old, my mother and I were at a car dealership. We were a few hundred dollars apart in the price that the dealer was asking.

My mother said to the dealer, "Well, I appreciate all of your efforts, but I just don't have any more money. We scraped everything together that we could, so I guess we'll just have to wait." She got up and started to leave.

Meanwhile, I'm sitting there like mom, "Please, I want the car!" She gave me one of those looks like, "Don't even try it."

With that I got up and, of course, the car dealer then said, "Well, wait a minute. Here's what we can do." To make a long story short, we got the car at the last price my mother put on the table.

Monica: It's amazing what you can learn from your parents as a child, even though sometimes as a child you really don't pay attention. Once you become an adult, you realize what they were trying to do for you.

Greg: Monica, I have reflected back on a lot of negotiation insights and lessons that I received from my mother. I never understood that those thoughts were implanted in my subliminal mind and would be released in many different environments as I negotiated with folks throughout the world. I never realized it then, but they've come back many times as I have negotiated throughout my life.

Monica: How did you perfect your skill?

Greg: Number one is practice. Number two is learning everything about strategies, tactics, and probing. I have to probe to find out how a strategy is supposed to work and what happens when I use it in a certain environment. I've been working 30+ years or so as a professional negotiator. In honing my skills, I have watched the reactions of people applying certain strategies. At the same time, I also teach people in training environments to read body language. So, when you couple understanding the strategies and tactics to implement an effective negotiating session with how to read and interpret body language, it becomes a very dynamic duo. You can truly get inside someone's head.

You don't take advantage of them, but you understand what the particular situation requires. When you couple reading body language with negotiation skills, it becomes a very interesting concept from which one can become a much better negotiator.

I practiced over the years. I went through all kinds of courses, read all kinds of materials, and then applied what I learned in real-life environments. I honed and perfected my skills as I negotiated on behalf of clients and large corporations.

Monica: Would participating on a debate team, becoming a member of a speakers' association, or joining an organization such as Toastmasters improve one's negotiation skills?

Greg: It can. I happen to be a past president of the New Jersey chapter of the National Speakers' Association. When you know how to convey your sentiment succinctly, that can give you an advantage. But, at the same time, you also have to know how to match the modality of the person with whom you're negotiating so you can increase the bonding process.

For example, if you're talking with someone from the South and you're from the North, you should instinctively know as a good negotiator that you do not necessarily want to speak as fast as you possibly can because you may lose that person. That person may not trust you simply because of the way you are speaking. Instead, you want to match the pace and tone of the other individual.

You don't want to mock them, but you want them to start to subliminally think and feel, "Wow, I like this person. This person is a lot like me." People have a tendency to like someone like themselves.

Monica: Why do you believe some people give in so quickly when they're attempting to negotiate a deal?

Greg: Number one, they fear not knowing what to do. Number two, they have not prepared succinctly enough to understand what they want from the negotiations.

If you're looking for $100,000, but you know you can live with $75,000, you have a bracket. You have a medium of $100,000 to $75,000. Then, throughout the negotiation you get to $125,000, and the other negotiator is either beginning to become squeamish or gives you non-verbal signals that you're a little too close to the edge. If you keep pushing, you may lose the whole deal.

When people don't understand where they are in the negotiation, they may be fearful to even attempt to negotiate. A lot of people don't like to negotiate. They feel as though it's going to make them look cheap. But as my mother said when I was a kid, "Wouldn't you rather have more of your money than somebody else?" The answer to that is a definite yes.

People need to become more aware of the negotiation process. There's a whole realm of steps that one goes through in order to perfect a very good and proper negotiation outcome. Most people do not know that and that's the reason why they're somewhat afraid to enter into negotiations.

Monica: Is negotiating similar to or the opposite of selling?

Greg: It can be either, depending upon where you are in the process. You're always negotiating, so you are selling yourself. But to the degree that you oversell yourself, you run the risk of losing the whole deal. When one comes into an environment, people are starting to make judgments about who you are and what they may be able to get from you based upon what they're seeking through you.

As soon as they start going through that process, you then have to meet their expectations or set the expectations by which they will measure you. They will grade you based on what you have to offer. From that perspective you are selling yourself. But the buyer also helps set the agenda about what you're supposed to be selling. One has to understand that whole process when you're negotiating because as people are viewing you, you are viewing them. There's that exchange going back and forth to make the sale palpable to everyone involved.

Monica: Let's say both parties want the best deal. How do you know when you have the best deal?

Greg: It goes back to bracketing. Look at what you're seeking from the outcome that you want. Let's say hypothetically, you're at the $100,000 mark already. You have what you're looking for in the negotiation, and yet you sense there is still more on the table. You could start going for more, and the other person says, "I'll give you $120,000 if you give me XYZ."

To the degree that that person is looking for that extra $20,000, you can say yes. You could make a counter offer and say, "I tell you what. If you give me the $125,000, I could give you part of what you're looking for." What you're doing with that whole strategy is setting the expectations. You're not going to get everything, but you may come close to receiving everything.

You could also employ a strategy whereby you say, "Since we have future negotiations coming about, I will give this to you if you will make sure that I get number one consideration for X, Y, Z in the future." Again, you walk away very happy.

Meanwhile, the negotiator is going, "Wow! I didn't expect to get that." There are all kinds of strategies you can employ as you go through the negotiation process.

Monica: Does a person's physical appearance play a role in winning or losing negotiations?

Greg: Oh, yes. Winning and losing is truly a matter of perception, so that's something that also has to be managed. The way you present yourself indicates to the other negotiator something that you have in the form of your persona. If you go into a Mercedes dealership, you don't want to project the fact that you have all the money in the world and you're willing to pay any price. So you may consider dressing down. You have to match the mood that you're trying to set with the style of dress that you actually convey.

Monica: Is there a major difference between how you negotiate on a personal level versus a business level?

Greg: Yes. Let's use a romantic environment first. First of all, the other individual knows you, your mannerisms, and your style much better than a business associate. Therefore, you may say something like, "Well, you know, this is not going to work."

And the other individual may say something like, "Whatever you're trying, it's not going to work. I know what you're doing," and then you have to use a different approach.

If you wish to get someone in a romantic environment or get that individual to do more of what you're looking for, you may have to prime the pump a little more than in a business environment. You would react differently in a business environment than you would in a romantic environment or a personal relationship that wasn't romantic.

Monica: You say to negotiate successfully do not argue with an idiot. What are some key points to identifying idiots?

Greg: First of all, you always want to qualify someone based on what you're seeking from the negotiation.

Going back to that $100,000 situation, you can say something like, "Can you ballpark a salary that I might be able to get from working in XYZ environment?"

The person says, "Well, $50,000 is the most you can get."

You say, "Well, how can I reach the $100,000 range given the fact that my base would be $50,000?"

He can come back and say, "Fifty thousand is all you're going to be able to get. You're not going to be able to get anything else."

Well, right away you start getting cues by the behavior of that individual. You might think, "Maybe I shouldn't even waste my time going into this environment because this person may be having an off day."

If that's the case, you can probe more gently by saying, "I'm sorry. I didn't mean to irritate you. I was just trying to understand how I could add more value to your environment and receive what it is that I am seeking."

The person comes back and says, "Well, I told you it's only $50,000. Are you stupid?" After that, you exit. There's nothing further. You're out of there.

Monica: I would imagine that there are many different things that one must keep in mind when negotiating. Is there one common denominator or one specific thing that applies every time?

Greg: Actually no. You can negotiate with the exact same person over the exact same thing in a different environment throughout a different day and the variables will change. You have to pay attention to not only how the person conveys his or her sense of it through their body language and match up your verbiage, but you also have to understand where they are mentally in the negotiation process. What works today may not necessarily work tomorrow because a change, however subtle, may have occurred. You can't go in with the same game plan thinking, "This is what I've always used, so it's always going to work."

Monica: Do you think anyone can become a successful negotiator?

Greg: The answer is a definite yes. Again, you have to understand the nuances that go into making a successful negotiation. Understand you will never win every negotiation. You may try your best to come as close as you possibly can, but given certain circumstances that you're not aware of you may be thwarted. If that's the case, you have to know when to back out because the more time you commit to a negotiation, the more you become ingrained in it. One ploy may be to get the other negotiator to invest more, while psychologically knowing that that negotiator is going to become worn down over time and will become susceptible to accepting less than what he was seeking.

Monica: When negotiating, how many counteroffers should you have in reserve?

Greg: Depending upon the circumstances, you can have multiple counteroffers in hand. But you want to apply them in a judicious manner. You do so based upon the circumstances. Going back to that $100,000 situation, the other negotiator says, "I can give you $90,000." That's a lot different than, "I tell you what. I can give you $90,000."

In the latter situation, you might come back with a counteroffer of, "If I could." Notice I preface it by saying "if" because that allows you to back out if the other party doesn't mean what they're saying. "If I can do this at $90,000, might I have an additional $20,000 in expenses?"

You always want to have something that can add up to at least what you're looking for or something that overshoots what you would be getting if the other party gave it to you. In this case, it would be the $100,000 that you were asking for.

Hypothetically you can say, "If I settle for the $90,000, can I get an extra $20,000 for expenses, a car, and a house at company expense? I would also like to have my children attend private school paid for by the company."

You keep building and the other person says, "Never mind. You've got the $100,000." Again, it's all about the tactic you wish to employ and how you present and position your counteroffers.

Monica: What is your view on the current state of the economy? How can the U.S. negotiate with other countries to improve our economic status? Would you say that our ability to survive as a nation depends on negotiations with other countries? Would negotiation be a major part of our getting out of the situation that we're in?

Greg: The answer is a definite yes. The United States is in a precarious situation right now. The dollar has lost its prestige against other currencies around the world. Our debt is also playing an important part in how other countries view us. To the degree that we appear to be strong and can pull ourselves out of this quagmire, we can present ourselves and position ourselves differently than if we went hat in hand to say, "You have to help us out."

China, one of our greatest partners who covers much of our debt, does not want to see us default. They have a vested interest in the United States becoming financially better. At the same time, China would not want the U.S. to become so financially set that they would have the U.S. become a threat in other parts of the world. Again, it's the give-and-take of negotiations. These negotiations are going on between not only the U.S. and China but also among other entities and other countries around the world. How the U.S. positions and presents itself plays a major role in what the U.S. can do.

Monica: Once both parties agree on the deal that has been made, what can you do to ensure that the other party does not back out of the deal?

Greg: First of all, you want to make sure that both parties understand what is coming forth from the agreement. You also want to make sure that the other party is not only in agreement but is also satisfied with the outcome. Congratulate the other individual on being fair and equitable. Be sincere. If the person was fair and equitable, say so. If the person was tough, say so. You give that person a comment that indicates you understand that you have been in a negotiation with an individual who understands the process and who knows what he wants. You can say something like, "Boy, oh boy. You really did get a good deal out of me."

Be humble in appearance while you congratulate the other individual. Tell the other individual what your expectations are for what is to occur next. You can say, "So now that we have concluded this deal, the product is going to be delivered on the 30th of the month. We will receive payment by the 15th of the month. If there are any maintenance requirements that are attached to this agreement, we will address any such actions within a 24-hour time period." Go over the final agreement, listen to the words that come back, and observe the body language.

If there is an incongruity between the words, the actions, and the body language, observe the body language more. If you sense that this individual may have any inkling of looking for a back door, as we call it in negotiations, you address that immediately. You can gently probe and ask, "Well, I heard you say yes, but you shook your head no. Which is it?"

The person may say, "Oh, I'm sorry. The answer really is yes." Now if they're saying yes while they are motioning toward you and waving their hands as if to say go away, there is an incongruity and you want to address that point. Watch the body language while they are saying what they are conveying to you.

Monica: How do you actually prepare for negotiations? You know you have this opportunity for a deal that's coming up. How do you prepare your mindset for it?

Greg: First of all, gather your background information. Find out everything that you can about the target with whom you will be negotiating as soon as you possibly can. For example, why are they negotiating? Why are they negotiating with you? What other resources can they bring to this situation that might allow them to have leverage? What resources do you have that you could use as leverage? What will the other individual do if they can't close the deal with you? How much time do they actually have to close the deal? Where else can they go to get additional assistance and time to save the deal? What happens if they can't get the deal? What happens if they don't have sufficient resources to get the deal? Who else can they align themselves with?

There is a conglomerate of questions that you need to ask yourself and be able to answer. After that, you want to map the course the negotiation may take and have alternative courses if you have to renew the negotiation. You also have to know how to get back on the path in order to have a successful outcome. If you put all of those thoughts and plans together, you will act upon what you have to do.

It will be like a chess game where you are thinking three, four, five moves ahead. If they do X, and you thought they were going to do Y, you have a contingency plan in place to address X as opposed to Y. That's how you put your whole negotiation scenario together. That's how you become more successful with the outcome you're seeking.

Monica: What do you enjoy most about helping others perfect their negotiating skills?

Greg: People can get a lot more out of life if they know how to ask for things and the timeframe in which to ask for them. In my negotiation training sessions, one of the tasks that I give during a lunch or dinner break is to have participants ask for something for free, no matter what environment they're in during that break period. Then I will have them come back and tell the rest of the class what they were able to get and how they went about doing so. I have them commit to that exercise to show them it's a lot easier than you think to simply ask for things. Those are some of the tactics that I use to enhance the knowledge level of people, especially in the United States. We have the tendency to see a price, think it is etched in stone, and we won't challenge it.

You can ask anybody for a price reduction if you're buying. There are all kinds of tactics you can use. What if the person says no? You will not die. Life will go on. One of the tactics that I talk about is buying something at a discounted price. If the person says, "No. I'm sorry. That's just too low. I can't accept it."

One thing you can say is, "I will give you $40,000 for this $65,000 car."

The person says, "Are you crazy? No. I would never do that."

You say, "No problem. I'm going to leave my business card with you. If you come upon a situation whereby you would like to accept this offer, let me know. Thank you very much." Turn and walk away.

Suddenly, it's the end of the month and the person at the car dealership realizes "Oh, my gosh. I need to sell a few more cars. This person made this offer. Let me go back and call them." There are all kinds of tactics and strategies you can employ.

Monica: Do you target a specific group of people with your training?

Greg: I train entrepreneurs because I have a real soft spot for them because I've been one since 1993. I also teach in corporate environments. Obviously, those are two different environments with two different mindsets. When I'm teaching in the corporate environment, I understand that those individuals are working for a larger entity. They may be a little laxer with what they will give in the form of leeway versus a small business owner who has to make sure that their bottom line is as sharp as it possibly can be. So, I train differently in each environment while at the same time making sure that I touch the bases for which anyone can become a successful negotiator.

Monica: Can you tell me a little about your latest book?

Greg: It's titled *Negotiate: Afraid Know More*, and "No" is spelled K-n-o-w. It goes back to the point that a lot of people are afraid to negotiate. They're afraid because they don't know everything that they should. I wrote the book initially as a result of presentations I had made and trainings that I had been involved in. I found that it became a bestseller simply because of the knowledge that it contained and what people could get from it. It covers strategies, tactics that one can employ in different environments, and how to read and decipher body language in order to strengthen one's negotiation abilities.

Everyone needs to know how to negotiate because we are always negotiating in every environment that we are in. Why not enhance your skills because you're doing it anyway? Why not become better at it and see how you can achieve more in life?

Monica: In parent-to-child situations, is that a good reason to learn negotiation skills?

Greg: Yes, but from whose perspective? The child or the parent? We are truly born negotiators.

Your mother commands, "No, you can't have such and such."

The child asks, "Why not?"

The mother says, "Because I don't want it to spoil your appetite."

The child can rebut, "Well, that's OK. I'll still be able to eat later."

You have these rebuttals that you come back with automatically. But as we become adults, we learn not to ask why not. It's not appropriate in certain environments, and we start to dumb ourselves down.

If we were to allow ourselves to act like kids sometimes when we're negotiating, we could end up achieving more throughout any negotiation. People will sit on their hands without trying to negotiate in certain situations because they're afraid of either losing what that they've already gained. They don't know what tactics to use. They don't want to be perceived as a buffoon or something worse. Thus, they won't even make an effort.

Parents and children truly learn from one another as they're going through the negotiation process. The mother finally gets fed up and says, "Go ask your father."

The kid says, "Daddy, Mommy told me to ask you if it's all right to have the ice cream that I'm getting ready to get."

Monica: They even know how to word it.

Greg: Exactly. The kid positions it as if it's a done deal. We lose those tendencies as we become older because we become more refined, whatever the heck that is.

Monica: I'll ask you what may seem like an odd question. As the master negotiator, what legacy would you like to leave?

Greg: That is an easy one. People of the world have become better at understanding the intrinsic value that they possess in selling themselves as a result of being able to negotiate. People in the United States do not negotiate as rigorously as people throughout other parts of the world. We in the United States need to catch up. We could stretch our resources voluminously if we would learn how to negotiate better. That's the legacy that I wish to leave.

Section 8

Public Relations

7 Key Steps to Creating a Great Press Release

Public relations consultant Dana Humphrey, owner of Whitegate PR, shares advice on how to create a press release that will attract media attention for your business.

Public Relations Expert Helps Entrepreneurs Get in the Spotlight

Helping people spread good news about their life's endeavors is Dana Humphrey's passion, and she has turned her passion into a successful business. Connecting and building relationships is her expertise. As a public relations expert, Humphrey is helping entrepreneurs, small business owners, and others spotlight their accomplishments, products, and services. She enjoys connecting with people so much that she was inspired to start her company, Whitegate PR.

Humphrey has an advantage that most public relations experts don't have. She's traveled to over 45 countries and has lived in five of them. "Being able to travel and connect with people from various backgrounds and languages definitely helps," she says. "I speak French and Spanish which helps me in my day-to-day life as a PR consultant. It gives someone who speaks French or Spanish confidence that I can better connect with them when I speak their language."

She is also using her gift as a natural-born leader to take on other roles within her community. Humphrey's recent community leadership roles include serving on the We Are Booming Board of Directors in 2011, being a member of the PRSA-NY International Volunteer Committee in 2009, and giving her ideas as a guest advisor for Ideablob in 2009. In 2010 and 2011, she served on the ACS Queens Board of Directors. The past year, she was an associate board member of the American Cancer Society in Brooklyn. In this interview with *Exceptional People Magazine*, Humphrey shared helpful advice and tips on how to create a great press release.

Monica: You've had a unique opportunity to travel to over 45 countries and you've also lived in five countries. What inspired your quest for traveling? Have you been able to use that in your profession as a PR consultant?

Dana: Absolutely. I think that being a traveler can help everyone in their careers. It helps you become a well-rounded person and understand different cultures and different people better. My parents were the main reason for my travel. I was born in Canada, and then my family moved from Cameroon, Africa to London, England. I grew up in London. My sister was born there and then we moved to California. Along the way we traveled and visited other countries. Once that travel bug gets in you, it never really goes away. I've traveled alone, with friends, for work, and for pleasure ever since. My family and I continue to travel together as well.

Monica: How are you able to use that experience to help change lives through your work?

Dana: Public relations is about connecting with other people. It's all about developing relationships and maintaining them. Being able to travel and connect with people from various backgrounds and languages definitely helps.

Monica: As a PR consultant, your area of focus is mainly the pet industry. Why did you focus on that particular industry?

Dana: The pet industry is my background. When I graduated from San Diego State University, my first two positions were doing PR and marketing at a wine company and then for a pet boutique. Now that I'm out on my own, we specialize in consumer products and services specifically in the pet industry. We also have a couple of wine clients as well.

Monica: You also specialize in small and large businesses, artists, authors, and nonprofits. Can you share some key points about how entrepreneurs and business owners can use public relations as a way to effectively help them promote their businesses?

Dana: From time to time I teach marketing boot camp courses or guerilla marketing tactics for small business owners. I'm really passionate about helping them to come up with low-cost or cost-effective solutions to market their business on a grassroots level. I really enjoy sharing with other people so that they can do it for themselves. It often turns out that a business owner wants to outsource that side of the business. At the end of the day, some people just don't want to do the marketing themselves and that's where I come in.

Monica: Many business owners and entrepreneurs are not familiar with how to write a press release. They don't know what should be included in a press release. Can you offer some tips on what would be considered a great press release?

Dana: A great press release is going to be something that's newsworthy and time worthy. If you're launching something or if you have something really exciting to share, then you want to write a press release. You don't want to write a press release just for the sake of having one. You really want to find a unique angle to put the press release together in a way that's going to be exciting and newsworthy.

As a PR person or as someone who wants to promote your business, you want to make the reporter's job as easy as possible. If you write a press release that has a hot title, a great story line, or includes great statistics and great quotes, it's much more likely to be picked up because the reporter or journalist doesn't have to do so much additional research. You've already put it out there for them. Here are a few elements of a good press release:

- Place your logo somewhere on the press release. Usually the top left corner is a good place.

- List your media contacts. It could be your company contact or the PR person. List their phone numbers and e-mail addresses.

- Include a headline. Focus your energy on creating a great title that's interesting and really announces whatever you're trying to release.

- Add your location. I'm here in New York, so press releases that I write would come from New York. If you're in California, you can put Santa Barbara, California and add the release date.

- Begin with a really good bit of information, whether it's a statistic, a trend, or something really interesting.

- Quote an expert in the industry or the CEO of the company.

- Have a section that has boilerplate information about the company with the website address at the bottom.

- To signal to the reporter that the press release is complete, put three pound signs (###) at the very bottom. This lets the person know this is the end of the release.

Monica: I've heard that press releases are best if they are one page.

Dana: If you are launching something that is very detailed and very expensive, it might be a three-page press release. It just depends how much information you have. I don't follow page rules. You want to keep it concise and tight. If you can fit it to one page, great. But if you have a lot of information to share and it's as streamlined as possible but it still takes two or three pages, that's fine, too. Just make sure it includes all critical information.

Monica: What do you enjoy most about being a marketing and PR consultant?

Dana: It's very exciting to get a media hit. It's still exciting every time it happens. When you get confirmation from a newspaper, magazine, or TV show that your client is going to be featured, it's that rush of "Yes! We're going to be featured!" My favorite part is being able to call them with exciting news that they are going to be featured in one of their target places or in a place that's really going to help their business.

Monica: I realize that public relations is an important part of the overall marketing plan for any business. But how important is public relations to a business?

Dana: It's essential. The idea of "build it and they will come" doesn't work anymore. In this day and age, people are getting thousands of messages every day. You have to be part of the mix. If your competitors are doing a better job of marketing their products than you, you can have a superior product but if no one knows about it, it doesn't really matter. Brand awareness, public relations, and being a trusted source in the field, is essential for almost any business. Being prepared for any kind of crisis in your industry and having a public relations strategy in place is also a critical part of public relations.

We are a member of the Public Relations Society of America, the professional association for public relations practitioners. I think that is important because a lot of people don't understand what public relations is and what a PR practitioner does. This is a professional association that tries to communicate this to the public and continues to push the boundaries of traditional PR. They have something called Accredited Public Relations (APR), which is something that I am working on this year. After you have been practicing public relations for over five years, you can take a test to gain your APR. I hope to achieve this goal within the next year.

Monica: You consider yourself to be a natural-born leader and a go getter. You have served on a few boards and you are associated with some wonderful organizations.

Dana: I'm very proud to be on the board of the American Cancer Society of Brooklyn. I also recently participated in the New York City triathlon to raise money for leukemia. This is something that I'm really passionate about. I do a lot of charity runs and half marathons to raise money for different organizations.

I'm also on the board of directors for a group called We Are Booming. This is an interesting project that looks at the baby boomer generation. This group recognizes that in the next 18 years there will be over 70 million baby boomers in the United States. Turning 65 is no longer a symbol of retirement. Today, a number of people who are 65 are not able to retire. They may be beginning a third or second career. I'm on a board to help celebrate aging and bring awareness to the baby boomer generation.

Get in the Spotlight: Additional PR Tips

Whenever you're communicating with the media always make sure that you answer the following questions:

Who? (Who is the news about and who needs to see it?)

What? (What is the news or the message?)

Where? (Where will the news affect the public? Locally, globally, regionally?)

When? (When will this news occur? This will also determine when you need to say it.)

Why? (Why is it important to the public? Is it related to something educational? Is it a public service message?)

How? (How will you present the message and how will it affect those you're trying to reach?)

Your press release is not considered complete until you have included these six important items. If you're sending a press release directly to specific media outlets, always remember to follow-up on occasion with the correct contact person. They may not have an immediate interest in your subject but may want to cover it later on.

"One important key to success is
self-confidence. An important key
to self-confidence is preparation."

Arthur Ashe

Section 9

125

Inspiration and Self-Empowerment

3 Key Elements to a Balanced Life

Performance training expert Tom Ziglar, CEO of Ziglar Corporation, shares powerful insights about business, personal, and professional success.

Zig Ziglar. The name is unmistakable and the vision behind it is powerful.

Decades ago, a young man by the name of Zig Ziglar had a well-defined vision and purpose that would eventually impact the lives of more than a quarter billion people, both personally and professionally. He built a company, The Ziglar Corporation, which provides professional development and performance training to corporations and individuals. The success of his empire was built on a solid foundation of impeccable ethics, integrity, caring, and sharing his knowledge with all mankind. As one of the world's iconic businessman, Ziglar's impact on history will live on forever.

After decades of touching lives in countless ways, Zig Ziglar passed the baton to his son, Tom, who is now leading the company into new territories. With the popularity of the Internet, social media, and other media platforms, the Ziglar Corporation has the capability to affect more lives than ever before.

The company's philosophy of building strong characters, positive attitudes, and enhancing skills hasn't changed, but the lives that these values impact have changed dramatically. The publisher of *Exceptional People Magazine* was thrilled to speak with CEO Tom Ziglar about his thoughts on success and his vision for the company. The Zig Ziglar empire lives on and his son Tom Ziglar is at the helm.

Monica: What do you think of your father's remarkable achievements and the impact he's had on millions of lives through the years?

Tom: Every time I look back, it amazes me. I don't know how many miles he traveled, but I would guess it's probably well over ten million miles. He's spoken to millions of people, and he's written many books. That's what gets the press, but now we're getting letters and they all have a consistent theme. The theme is, "Mr. Ziglar, I saw you speak twenty years ago. When I met you, it was like I was the only person in the room."

Dad had this ability to really focus in, even if it was just for a minute, and recognize each person. That's what they remember. They don't talk about his speeches or awards. They talk about how he made them feel when he spent just a minute with them one on one. These are people we don't know at all. Every week we get a letter like that.

It's one thing to have notoriety, celebrity, and stage presence. It's another thing when people repeatedly say, "Your dad is the real deal one on one," or "The reason he changed my life is because of the brief conversations we had. Not just this great talk." We're seeing a ripple effect of all these people he's impacted.

Monica: What was it like growing up "the Ziglar way"?

Tom: My Dad was a pretty normal dad, but he was always extremely consistent. I knew he wanted me to do the best at whatever I chose to do. There wasn't pressure to be a certain person or to do a certain thing.

He wanted me to do whatever I wanted to do as well as I could with character and dignity. He's always been there when I needed to talk. Even though he traveled unbelievable amounts of time, he was almost always home on the weekends. We played a lot of golf and spent a lot of time together.

When we were on the road, we would often be interrupted by someone at dinner. People would come to us and say, "Mr. Ziglar, I've always wanted to meet you." Then they would tell their story about how Dad impacted them. That interruption never gets old.

Monica: In what ways has your father inspired and motivated you to become the person you are today?

Tom: His stories, his life principles, and the qualities he stands for are embedded in my DNA because he would tell me these things as I was growing up. When you're young, you don't always understand how important it is. Now that I'm older, I'll start doing something new or different and think, "Oh, wow! I'm brilliant. I've figured this out." Then, all of a sudden, I think, "Dad's been saying that for 40 years."

One of my favorite quotes from my Dad is, "You are who you are and what you are because of what's gone into your mind. You can change who you are and you can change what you are by changing what goes into your mind."

In a lot of ways, I'm a product of all the things he spoke into me. He was putting the good things in. Those good things included the affirmations, the discipline, and telling me that character, honesty, hard work, and discipline are the keys to success. All of those things can make you the right kind of person that has long-term success. There aren't any shortcuts.

As I get older, I realize how true it is. The message for hope for anybody out there is regardless of what's gone into your mind in the past, your family relationships you had at home, or how difficult your situation is, you can proactively choose what to put into your mind and you can choose to start associating with people who can build you up rather than tear you down.

Monica: You are now the CEO of the company. When the baton was passed to you to run the company how did your life change? What impact did it have on your life?

Tom: When I was in college, I thought I was going to be a professional golfer. After college, I traveled for a year and played golf. I also got married and started working part-time at the company. After doing that, I realized how good the players on tour really are. I realized I had a lot of work to do to get there. About that same time, I moved from the warehouse and production into sales at the company. I fell in love with sales, serving people, and selling our different programs.

I did that for about 10 years. It was a good thing for everybody else here that I had that experience before I got promoted. I came into my current role almost 15 years ago. All the things Dad spoke into my life prepared me. When you take on a responsibility that you've never done before, there's a lot of learning that comes with it.

His encouragement along the way helped tremendously as we did different things. I couldn't believe that I didn't miss golf. Then one day I started reading the letters we'd get from people whose lives had changed. That's what really floats my boat. When we get a testimonial from somebody because of something we've done either on the personal development level or at the corporate level, that's what keeps me going. There's no greater joy than having an impact in someone else's success.

Monica: I know your father is proud of you, your achievements, and your leadership role in the company. Has he given you much advice over the years?

Tom: For the last 7 to 10 years, he really hasn't given me any kind of corporate direction advice. But he's always there to provide feedback for anything or any questions I might have. He loves speaking and writing books. Of course, he's 85 and he's not traveling and speaking anymore. He has always said, "I'm good at writing and speaking, and you're good at running the company."

Monica: In a world that is changing so quickly, what is your vision for the future of the Ziglar Corporation? How do you plan to continue to implement your father's philosophy?

Tom: We've done a number of things. One of the most visible things that we've been working on is a program that we've called Success 2.0. We have a studio in our offices and we can do live training that we film in the studio and broadcast over the Internet. For example, we've had over a thousand people in probably 30 or 40 different countries watching a live training session.

We offer the Success 2.0 live webcast for free. If they like it, we ask people to join a membership program where they can have access to over 200 hours of our content that's stored online. With Success 2.0 and digital downloads, we can sell a program in India just as easy as we can in Oklahoma.

For us, the market and the business has changed significantly because of technology and the economy. But the actual number of people and our ability to reach them has grown exponentially because we can get it out much more cost effectively.

We also specialize in in-house training for small- to medium-sized businesses. We also provide training for large corporations specifically in the areas of sales, presentation skills, and customer service. Any organization that needs sales development and training, that's what we do. We don't look at it as a "one and done." We look at it as a program and a process.

We tell people that we're in the transportation business. We help you get from where you are to where you want to be. When it comes to being effective in learning something in sales, it's not a "one and done" event. It's a process. We might do a two-day class, a conference call, a webcast, online learning, follow-up training, and coaching. All these things are combined together. The idea is for you to get from where you are to where you want to be. This is what Dad calls persistent consistency. You've got to improve in different areas every day. It's not a radical one-time change. It is minute changes every day.

The downside to doing a one-day or two-day class is you learn a totally new process, then you go out and try it, and when you don't have any success, you abandon it. That's the way we are. We don't like change. If you learn a new process, try it, come back, and get feedback, when you do that type of process, the outcomes totally change. They are predictable and incrementally better. At the end of the year, you get dramatic results. That's how we teach our programs.

Monica: Speaking of sales, how different is selling online versus selling in person?

Tom: The Internet has made it easy to reach out and touch a lot of people. The only problem is that it's made the seller-prospective buyer relationship very transactional. People think that because they're doing a good job reaching out to their audience that it's actually going to result in sales. But even online, people are looking for relationships. Many times online, people go straight for the sale. In order to build a relationship online, first you have to establish trust and that trust comes from providing value. It could be a blog post, a free webcast, an e-book, a free download, a newsletter, or a podcast. Any combination of these things builds trust.

You want to build a happy medium by providing value online through social media and the Internet. Then you want to quickly move it to a one-to-one relationship. That relationship might come from e-mail, a direct message on Twitter or Facebook, a phone conversation, or a face-to-face meeting. Selling today is no different than it's been before. Dad has a great quote that says, "If they like you, they'll buy from you one time. If they trust you, they'll buy from you over and over again."

Monica: You have several family members working at The Ziglar Corporation. What would you say are some important key differences and points to consider when running a family-owned business?

Tom: In a traditional business where your corporate goal is profitability, your job is to equip your team with the skills, knowledge, and tools to get it done. You lead them with integrity. You cast a vision for where you're going. At the end of the day, you have to make business decisions that reward the people who are providing the most value and input to the organization.

When you're working with family, all of those things are still true, but you try harder to make sure your family members are in the roles that are best suited for their personality and style. You have more leverage of creating a hybrid position for family members so they can really expose their strengths.

When you think about the businesses that reinvent themselves, they are most creative when they get people who are good and invent new positions in those businesses for those people. A family business is very similar in its success to a traditional business that's figured out how to leverage the strengths of their best people.

The old-fashioned business owners who say, "No. This is your role. This is all that you can do," they are struggling right now. The old ways of running a traditional business are going away. Successful, family-owned businesses go the extra length to provide the right position in the company for the family member.

A great company should provide the best position for everyone who works there. If they're a valuable member of the team and they have some strengths, we need to figure out how to leverage those strengths. The boundaries that you've got to draw in a family are a little tougher. Sometimes you have a family member who doesn't have the passion to be in the business or they don't have the skill set to be there. That's when you have to carefully manage the family and business relationships. Sometimes that's hard. I tell people there's nothing better than working in a family business and there's nothing tougher than working in a family business.

Monica: Who is Tom Ziglar? Who is the man behind the corporation, both from a business and personal perspective?

Tom: My byline is, "Tom Ziglar—Pure and Simple." I like to simplify things as much as possible and I look at the pure approach from all aspects, physically, mentally, and spiritually. I am not a motivational and inspirational speaker. Dad is.

To be honest, I hesitated a long time before I began speaking. I felt like I needed to represent him in my style of speaking. What I've learned in the last four or five years is that's not true. I need to represent him in the character, the philosophy of what I speak about, and how I speak. But I had to find my own style. That's a lesson for anyone. You've got to be your own person and find your own passions. I'm quiet and I'm a thinker. Dad is known as an inspirational energizer bunny on stage. It's not my style.

Monica: Let's talk about your perspective on your Dad's philosophy for living a balanced life based on character, attitude, and skills. Lord Acton once said, "Character is tested by true sentiments more than by conduct. A man is seldom better than his word." From your point of view, how does one's character play a key role in living a balanced life?

Tom: Character is everything. If your long-term objective is to have a high level of success in finances and marriage, people should be talking about how much integrity you have. Without that, everything else crumbles. In our program, we have what we call a Wheel of Life. In this portion of the program, Dad talks about balance.

In the Wheel of Life, imagine that it has seven spokes that represent your personal, family, business, physical, mental, spiritual, and financial life. You rate yourself in each one of those categories on a scale of 1 to 10. In order for your ride in life to be smooth, each one of those spokes has to be the same length.

People get into trouble when they spend all their time in their business and their financial spokes and neglect their family and their physical spokes. Maybe your mental spoke is really good but you don't have any relationships on your personal side. You've got to consciously and purposely decide and choose to be balanced in every area of your life.

This is what I love about Dad. I'd say he's a mathematician. There are two math equations that he talks about that I love. In the first one he says, "I've done the math. I know I'm going to be dead a lot longer than I'm going to be alive." For many people, that's a spiritual wake-up call.

The other thing he says is, "You plus God equals enough." When he realized that there's a lot more out there and began looking at his life from a long-term, eternal perspective, that's when his whole life and career changed. His spiritual life took off and he became a Christian.

There's also the financial and personal spokes on the wheel. If you're money-driven, you could work 80 hours a week, die of an ulcer, and have nobody show up at your funeral. That's not successful either.

Balanced success is really in the Wheel of Life. When you work on every one of these things and the core of your character is based on integrity, you will have all the right things that will make you be the right kind of person. Dad calls it the "Be-Do-Have" philosophy. You've got to "Be" the right person before you can "Do" the right things. When you "Do" the right things, you will "Have" the rewards.

Monica: What about attitude?

Tom: Attitude is the fuel. Dad says, "A lot of people complain motivation doesn't last." His counterpoint to that is, "Well, neither does bathing. But if you bathe every day, you'll smell good and have more friends." You literally have to learn how to self-motivate yourself. You can do that by listening to or reading motivational and inspirational things on a daily basis.

Some people are confused by that. Dad does not say positive thinking will let you do anything. What he does say is positive believing will allow you to do everything better than negative thinking will. A positive attitude is critical, but it needs to be based on belief and belief comes out of your preparation. How do you prepare for this time? It's based on what you have read, who you have worked with, what you have learned, and what you have done in the past. My dad is a huge believer in motivation and attitude. But he also believes that it needs to be combined with skill, purpose, and belief that come through preparation.

Monica: It goes without saying that you must have the skills to be prepared to achieve the goals that you set for yourself.

Tom: When we talk about our training, we say you have to have will, skill, and refill. If you want to go to the next level, then you've got to have these three things. Will is simply the heart, the desire, the passion, the motivation, and the attitude to get it done. Skill is the process and the technique. It's also the hard learning, experience, and expertise. Refill means you have to work on the will and skill every day.

Monica: Personally, what does success mean to you?

Tom: Success is a number of things. From a spiritual standpoint, success means glorifying God in the process, not just in the end result. When I interact with people or when I do something, how I do it and why I do it, that's important. I can only control what I can do and how I do it.

Monica: What will it take for us as individuals to deal with and successfully overcome the economic challenges we face today?

Tom: If I were to advise somebody on what to do, I would first tell them to turn off all the negative input. The radio, the television, the newspaper—all the things that keep telling you that you can't do it. This also includes people that you work with and talk to.

Taking in that negative information does not solve one problem or help you get any closer to where you need to be. Take out as much of that as you can, and literally turn off the television and turn off the negative input. Dad says that the economy between our two ears is far more important than the economy that is outside. We can't control what's outside, but we can control what's between our ears.

If we have a dream or vision of what we want to do in our work or future endeavor, then we need to get rid of the negative input and start replacing it with positive input. What I say positive input, this is not just motivation and inspirational things. It's also the skill-based things as well. It's the knowledge you need to have in order to get to that next level. It's the relationships you need to develop. Every single day you focus on that and work a plan to get there. It's got to start with hope. The problem with our country right now is there are so many hopeless people. When you don't have hope, you won't do anything.

Here's a question that Dad used to ask when he would speak to audiences, "How many of you believe there's something in your personal, family, or business life that you could do in the next three weeks that would make things worse?" They'd all raised their hands. Then he'd ask, "How many of you here today believe there's something in your personal, family, or professional life that you could do to make things better in the next three weeks?" They'd all raise their hands. He'd just pointed out the reality and the fact that each one of us has the ability to make things either better or worse, and the choice is ours.

Monica: Absolutely. Life is all about choices.

Tom: When you own that, hope is born. When you own that, you can either sit there and do nothing or you can choose to reinforce your will and the skill in the right direction. When you own that choice of doing something different and better every day, hope will grow and you will find a way. We've got to create hope in ourselves and our fellow men and go after it. You have to take action. No one can think our way out of this economic situation. We've got to "act and do" our way out of it.

Monica: What words of advice can you offer small business owners and entrepreneurs to help them gain confidence to press forward?

Tom: Our country needs entrepreneurs and small business owners more than ever. Big business is not going to rescue this nation. It's going to be small business owners and entrepreneurs getting a little bit better in growing, hiring, and doing what they do best. It's always been that way. If you're an entrepreneur or small business owner, what an awesome place to be in. You've got a huge responsibility.

You owe it to yourself, your family, and everyone to do the right things to get there. That's where you practice the will, skill, and refill philosophy. You're filling your mind with the right things so you can have the right attitude, the right motivation, and the right desire. You're learning the right things to enhance and grow your business. That could be marketing, sales, or learning how to run your budget. There are tons of free resources on the web that will help you do that. Take inventory to see what you're good at and not good at. Get skills in the areas where you need improvement.

Monica: What legacy would you like to leave as CEO?

Tom: Dad has created such a philosophy. He's impacted so many lives. My role is to take that same philosophy and make it relevant for the next generation He'd be the first to tell you that he didn't invent the concepts he came up with. He was just very eloquent in how he spoke about them. Most of the principles come out of the Bible. He learned it from his mentors along the way. He has always had a special way of communicating them to people. I have my own passions for the business that are in line with Dad's character and philosophy. Some categories I'm stronger than he is and vice versa.

I want to make Dad's core message relevant to the next generation. I want to make it pure and simple by using technology to get the word out, meeting people where they are, and communicating ideas that change lives. It seems like it's intangible but it's not.

7 Keys to Achieving Wealth

"I definitely don't do what I do for the money. I do what I do because I think it's necessary."

"Is this the greatest value and benefit that I can deliver to the world? That is the question that I challenge everyone to wake up and ask themselves."

Business and wealth coach William R. Patterson, CEO of Warcoffer Capital Group, LLC, shares key elements to achieving wealth and business success.

A Mastermind at Helping Others Create Wealth

As children, we often asked our parents for things without regard to the cost. Remember how our parents responded? Many parents asked, "Do you know the value of a dollar?" Of course, most of us didn't. But by age 8, William Patterson's father made sure he understood. He received lessons of a lifetime on how to create wealth by making the right choices by following a "using what you had" philosophy and building on that.

His father refused to give him an allowance. Instead, he suggested that William purchase bulk candy and sell it at a lower cost than the local grocery store. This experience ignited Patterson's passion to become involved in business and it made him who he is today. This young lad knew he wouldn't need to ask his father for an allowance anymore.

"There were things that my father did to help me understand business principles, financial principles, and just life principles," Patterson says. "I grew up on the South Side of Chicago in a diverse neighborhood known as Hyde Park. It is probably famous now because of President Obama. I grew up seven to ten blocks from where he lived. There were many iconic figures in the neighborhood, including Muhammad Ali and Minister Louis Farrakhan. I lived among people from diverse cultures and backgrounds and I learned from those influences.

"I attended St. Ignatius College Prep High School. It was one of the best schools in the city. I also attended Murray Language Academy as a child, where I studied Japanese and had an opportunity to travel to Japan. As a young child, I learned that there was a whole world outside of my neighborhood. The trip provided an opportunity for me to learn about the Japanese culture and values. And not only from a financial perspective, but their concepts of family life, religion, and business. I learned to appreciate those things, and it gave me a fairly diverse perspective."

These experiences helped Patterson become a mastermind at helping others appreciate life and build wealth. He is leaving his mark of excellence throughout America and the world.

"Is this the greatest value that you can deliver to the world?" That is the question that he often asks of his clients. "Is there something that could have gotten you to your point of success faster?" His method of achieving success can help you.

Think about this for a moment. What is your greatest value? What is your life's passion and how can you develop it to create lasting wealth? What can you do or what skills do you have that will have a lasting impact on humanity? Those are questions that Patterson can help you answer.

His methodology for achieving success has had a lifelong impact on major corporations, small business owners, and individuals alike. His genius approach to wealth, success, and influence has benefited clients such as The Boeing Company, Morgan Stanley, CBS Radio, Intel Corporation, and countless others. Patterson has dedicated his life to helping people discover their true potential and fulfill their aspirations of achieving success.

Among his many achievements as CEO of the Baron Solution Group, he is ranked as one of the top business motivational speakers in America. Patterson is also a three-time award-winning lecturer who uses his signature Baron Solution Approach to coach, train, and motivate small business owners, executives, sales professionals, and investors.

The Baron Solution Group was founded by Patterson, D. Marques Patton, and Vicky Therese Davis. All three founders are also co-authors of the international best-selling business and personal finance book, *The Baron Son*. This book was featured in the Forbes Book Club and can be found in various translations around the world. His hard-won efforts in building a successful business have enabled him to interact with billionaires, Fortune 100 CEOs, presidential candidates, all of whom have endorsed him.

As chairman and CEO of the Warcoffer Capital Group, Patterson leads the company's corporate strategy, development consulting efforts, portfolio management, mergers, acquisitions, and divestitures. He has not only helped others turn dreams into reality, but he also uses his wealth of knowledge to help inspire young people and give them a sense of purpose. His passion is not to achieve wealth but to make a difference. Patterson graciously took the time to share his thoughts with the editor-in-chief of *Exceptional People Magazine*.

Monica: As a college student, you studied electrical engineering. What inspired you to move into the financial industry?

William: When I started off in electrical engineering, I was not one of the true engineers. I didn't begin electrical engineering because I was passionate about it. A lot of the "real" engineers were in the basement creating things and inventing things. That wasn't me.

I went into engineering because I was good in math and science. This was also something that my father encouraged me to do. Some of the things that we also teach as part of our youth programs is something called the Law of Expectation. My father instilled in me that I was good in math and science. I began to live up to that expectation, and math and science became very strong areas for me. That's how I ended up in the electrical engineering field.

My goal was to ultimately become the CEO of a Fortune 100 company. I figured one of the fastest ways to do that was to start with the technical route. Engineering was also one of those degrees where you would be considered a professional even with a bachelor's degree.

During this time, I had a number of really great mentors. These people influenced and encouraged me. One of my mentors was a gentleman named Chris Williams, head of the Williams Capital Group, one of the largest black investment banks on Wall Street.

I started to really understand what it took to make a business work. I was working on Wall Street at the time, but I later launched my own company. This is where I started a business that evolved into the Warcoffer Capital Group.

We looked at some of the strategies used on Wall Street. We looked at ethical strategies, unethical strategies, good strategies, bad strategies, and eventually developed the roadmap that became the Baron Solution. It was not about how to earn a few more dollars a month or how to become a millionaire. We focused on how to take an idea that you're passionate about, use that idea to dominate an industry niche, and create a legacy for future generations. That's what the Baron Solution is all about. For those who read the message in *The Baron Son*, there's also a concept of being a social entrepreneur. Not just using your skills to impact the bottom line, but also having a social impact.

It's no longer enough, particularly at this critical time in our history, for you to only be concerned about you and your money. You also have to look at the crisis that's happening internationally as far as global warming and extreme waste.

Monica: Oscar Wilde once said, "Success is a science. If you have the conditions, you get the results." What conditions are necessary for achieving success and wealth?

William: I think the first thing that is necessary is a roadmap. That roadmap can often come from a mentor, an advisor, or a coach. There's no point in reinventing the wheel if someone has been there before you.

The second thing is having a belief system that supports that idea of success. You have two different viewpoints of the world. You can view it from the point of scarcity or you can view it from the point of abundance. It's very important for most people to take a viewpoint of abundance and possibility as opposed to scarcity and lack.

That's one of the big differentiating factors that we found between our clients who achieve higher levels of success. They go into a situation believing that it's possible, even if that belief may be unwarranted based on how they're going to do it.

Expanding your belief system is essential. One of the reasons that so many people struggle is they don't think big enough. I always tell people whatever dream that you have, make it ten times bigger than you're currently thinking. You'll attract more attention and different types of people who are interested in what you are doing if you operate in wider and bigger arenas.

The third thing that is necessary is networking and having relationships that can get you to where you want to be. The right relationships can open a lot of doors. The Law of Significance says, "Nothing significant is ever accomplished alone."

We always talk about your network being a direct reflection of your net worth. But when you look at this chain of six degrees of separation, it's essential that you start to build those relationships. You may be able to pick up a phone and call Bill Gates or Oprah, but the question is, have you built the relationship that would make them want to help you? Being able to cultivate your network is big.

The fourth thing is leveraging those vehicles to get to your goal. If you're talking about financial success, then you're looking at real estate, the stock market, and entrepreneurship. If you're talking about some other means of success, you really want to look at the vehicles that the most successful people have used to get to that goal and you want to repeat that.

Knowledge and skills would be the fifth thing that you work on. I always encourage people to continue to learn. If you don't like reading, there are lots of audio and video materials out there. You should always continue to learn and upgrade your skills.

The sixth thing is getting the right tools. There are many great tools that will give you leverage and more time so you can accomplish more things. Investing in those tools can help you.

The last thing is taking action and doing the most important thing every day that will get you to your goal faster. If your goal is to build a million-dollar business, you have to go after the million-dollar deals or you have to go after enough small deals to get to a million dollars.

Success is a culmination of those seven things—the mentor, the belief system, the network, choosing the right vehicles, the knowledge and skills, the right tools, and taking action on the most important things every day. As we've found in our research in working with so many different entrepreneurs, these are the things that become the culmination of success.

Monica: Through the years, you've helped millions of people. What have you found to be the common denominator for why people don't achieve the financial success that they seek? Do they need to change something about themselves or the way they think?

William: It's definitely the way they think. Those seven points are what we call our seven millionaire success habits. Typically, if you go through that list, you will find the differences in the people who struggle financially.

For instance, if they don't have an advisor, they're just trying to reinvent the wheel. Let's say you just bought a piece of equipment, and it doesn't come with an instruction manual, how many hours are you going to sit there trying to figure out how this thing works? It's just not worth the time. When they look at the vision, they don't truly believe that they can change the condition of their life starting from where they are. They continue to procrastinate and do the small things.

You have entrepreneurs who have an idea, but they say, "I don't want to tell anyone about this idea." I'm not afraid to share ideas. This is one of the reasons why I coach on business matters. I feel like I have thousand-dollar or million-dollar ideas every day. If I give one away, great.

You want your idea to build wealth for other people. And the more wealth and the more value that you can create for other people, the more wealth that will eventually come back to you.

A lot of people have heard of the concept called Other People's Money (OPM). Well, instead of OPM, we teach a concept called Other People's Everything: their time, their money, their resources, their network. The leverage is the key. Using intelligence leverage and managing the risk is the key. Being able to put together a team where you can increase your productivity, value, and the number and magnitude of the problems you can solve will help you multiply your income. These are the things that are going to make a huge difference in your ability to improve your circumstances.

Monica: You have dedicated your life to helping others discover their true potential and fulfill their dreams, but do you sometimes get advice from others?

William: Absolutely. Everything that we talk about in the Baron Solution Group is an extension of everything that we teach.

Monica: How do you describe the impact that you have on peoples' lives every day?

William: We've been very fortunate to be able to get up every day and focus on solving problems for people. One of the things that we're most excited about is not just the financial impact that we can have on a company, but also their ability to employ others, create a better life, and develop a more sustainable existence for themselves, their families, and their businesses.

The businesses aspect is one of the things that a lot of people don't think about. If this business goes down and they're a supplier of parts for another business, their costs can go up. It could potentially bankrupt that other company. We try to help our partners and suppliers adopt more sustainable strategies. It helps to stabilize that business or potentially that small subset of the industry.

In the Baron Young Millionaires Program, we teach business and financial skills to students. We do a lot with the Sigma Gamma Rho Chapter and the Phi Sigma Chapter to teach financial literacy skills to teen mothers. Everything that we do is about creating a more sustainable existence where people can focus on the things that they love doing.

Monica: I'm sure you believe that social responsibility is key to corporate success.

William: Absolutely. Ultimately, I believe it does a great deal for your brand in terms of brand favorability and awareness when you do positive things. I always believe in appealing to a person's self-interest and a company's interest, as opposed to their sense of obligation, loyalty, or duty.

Monica: What does success mean to you personally?

William: Success for me is being able to get up, do something that I absolutely love every day, be able to help people, and leave that legacy. If you can do those three things, I think you are fairly successful.

Monica: If there is one key life lesson that you'd want people to absorb or to apply to their lives, what would it be?

William: It would be to solve problems. Solve more and larger problems because the more problems that you can solve, the greater your income, the greater impact you will have in the world, and the greater legacy you'll be able to leave.

Monica: As a person who has achieved extraordinary success and has also helped millions of others do the same, what is your overall view of life?

William: My overall view of life is that it's very short. In order for it to be meaningful, you need to leave a legacy. This is why I wake up every morning and I ask myself the question, "Is this the greatest value and benefit that I can deliver to the world?"

That is the question that I challenge everyone to ask themselves. If it's not, step up and pursue that passion. For some people, it's being a parent and they're doing it. I don't pass judgment and say you need to be running a multi-billion-dollar corporation to be successful.

I definitely don't do what I do for the money. I do what I do because I think it's necessary. I think it can help people. I focus on business and wealth building from the standpoint that it allows you to build some scalable systems where you can help more people.

"The truth is, publicity is not about being famous and it never has been. It's about building awareness, and becoming the go-to source that people trust. When you build trust, it leads to more customers, profits, and a higher level of influence that you can use to build exceptional partnerships in your business."

Monica A. Davis

Find Valuable Lessons in Life's Setbacks

Dynamic speaker, singer, and author Willie Jolley shares his story of how he turned a major setback into an amazing comeback and created a remarkable success story for others to learn from.

An Attitude of Excellence

When it comes to public speaking, he is a heavyweight. When it comes to motivation, he's a master at his game. When it comes to overcoming obstacles, he's a conqueror.

Willie Jolley shares something in common with some of the most renowned people in the world, including Margaret Thatcher, Nelson Mandela, and Colin Powell.

Named one of the Outstanding Five Speakers in the World, Willie has shared the spotlight with many extraordinary motivational speakers. He was inducted into the Speakers Hall of Fame by the National Speakers Association, joining other luminaries such as Ronald Reagan, Zig Ziglar, and Les Brown. In 2003, McDonald Corporation named him "A Black History Maker of Today."

These accolades did not come easy to Willie. He set himself up for success. He even wrote the book on it—*A Setback Is a Setup for a Comeback*. This book is a bestseller that has been translated into eight languages. He also authored *It Only Takes a Minute to Change Your Life*.

Even as a young boy, Willie had the entrepreneurial spirit. As a newspaper boy, he designed a distribution system that turned into one of Washington, D.C.'s most profitable routes.

Born and raised in Washington, D.C., this young lad had more on his mind than newspapers. He wanted to become a musician and singer. At the age of 15, he performed with a singing group called 98.6. The group became a local success. That opportunity led to more success in the music business where he became a background performer for jazz legend Jean Carne, a vocalist for Phyllis Hyman, and many others. Later as a solo act, Willie became one of Washington's most popular jazz performers, winning five consecutive Washington Area Music Association (WAMMIE) Awards for Best Jazz Vocalist and Best Entertainer.

As we often experience, life has a way of showing us that we were meant to do other things and that there's another purpose to our lives. In 1990, Willie was fired from his jazz club gig and replaced by a karaoke machine. One karaoke machine, however, didn't stop the show. He tried his hand at becoming a star and as he puts it, "I bombed royally."

Today Willie enjoys a career as a dynamic motivational speaker where he combines his extraordinary speaking skills with music. As a co-author of the bestselling book, *Go M.A.D. (Go Make A Difference)*, Willie encourages young people to achieve academic excellence.

What's his life's mission? To help people maximize their God-given talents and abilities so they can, "Do more, be more, and achieve more." Willie was gracious enough to share his thoughts with *Extraordinary People Magazine*.

Monica: At a young age, you had amazing musical talents. You signed your first record deal at the age of 17. Even at a much younger age, you dreamed of creating music that you could share with the masses. Where did your inspiration for the love of music come from?

Willie: My brother and I both were involved in music from early ages, but my talent didn't particularly come from my parents. They were not musically inclined. My grandparents, however, were musical, especially my grandfather. It must have skipped a generation because both my brother and I became very musical.

And at an early age, my father saw my interest in music. He allowed us to have guitar and other music lessons. I started with a guitar and moved to trumpet. My brother stayed with the guitar. Then I sang in the choir and was actively involved in music through elementary school, junior high, and high school. I played in the band from sixth grade on.

Monica: You often say that a setback is a setup for a comeback. When you attempted to become a music star, you were not successful at it.

Willie: I bombed royally. I could not have bombed any worse if I had planned it.

Monica: That was a major setback for you. How did you prepare yourself to turn that specific setback into a comeback to become the amazing speaker that you are today?

Willie: It was out of that setback that I learned some valuable lessons. The most important lesson that I learned was why I do what I do. I had gone to Nashville to be in a showcase for the Gospel Musical Association. Typically, the people who were involved in those showcases would get major record deals. I was there to impress everybody about how good I was so they would see the talent that I had, hoping that they would sign me to a major record deal. I thought that I would put out a record, it would become a hit, and I would become famous.

That experience, that bombing, gave me an opportunity to reflect afterwards and see what was really important. I realized that I am not here to impress people; I am here to inspire people. If I inspire people, 9 times out of 10 they would be impressed, but it doesn't work in the opposite direction. If you impress people, you won't always inspire them.

I realized that the larger message was to inspire and not impress. I started speaking after that experience. I would always reflect back to that time. When I get great opportunities to speak in front of large crowds, I'll say, "Don't forget why you are here."

Once I took that off of the table, then I had one singular goal—to inspire people. That goal took away a lot of the nervousness, apprehension, and trepidation. I was able to view people from another perspective. That's my job. If they are not impressed when this is over, then it is not a problem. But if they are not inspired, then I would be upset.

Monica: When you first began speaking as a professional, was there ever a time when you felt that you didn't do your best? If so, how did you deal with that?

Willie: There have been numerous times when I felt that I could have done better. I am my worst critic. I am always trying to get better. My mindset is that we should always have a one percent solution to success. For me that means that I should be one percent better every time I do what I do. I also had a challenge that tomorrow I can be better than I was today. I tell people, "When I really get this thing together, I am going to be good!"

Monica: Do you think anyone can become an effective speaker?

Willie: Yes. I believe that anybody can become an effective speaker and communicator.

Monica: What important elements must they have?

Willie: What happens if you have a person who can't talk or is mute? They can also become an effective communicator. The secret is training. That is why we have our speaker seminars so that we can help others become better and more effective communicators.

Monica: You inspire millions of people every day to live up to their potential. What do you think is the main reason why so many people don't succeed in their endeavors?

Willie: The main reason that people don't succeed is because they don't try. Most people think about it or talk about it, but they never actually move toward doing it. Statistics show that the majority of people who have an idea only think about it and never do it. They say, "I am going to one day," but they never do it. Studies show that most people who attempt to do something will have success in higher numbers than can be imagined.

The reason why most people don't achieve what they want is because it is hard. Achieving anything is hard. The second reason is because they don't have clearly defined goals. The third reason is because they don't have a big enough 'Why.' Your desire has to be strong to achieve your goals.

Monica: Do you consider yourself to be a perfectionist?

Willie: No. I don't even pursue it. I consider myself to be a student of excellence. I gave up a pursuing perfection a long time ago because perfection makes you crazy. Excellence is never ending. You can be perfect in bowling or something where you hit the bull's eye every time. But with perfection, there is nowhere to go. After you do that, what's left? Excellence says, "How can I better myself tomorrow?" or "How can I continue to get better so I can have greater opportunities?" I am always pursuing excellence.

Monica: Jose Marti once said, "Men are like stars. Some generate their own light while others reflect the brilliance that they receive." Are you one of those?

Willie: That is a good quote. I think I am a little bit of both. I think I generate a lot of my opportunities. When I was a singer, I was waiting for my break. But when I became a speaker, a positive thinker, and a critical thinker, I started saying, "I am not waiting for anyone. I am going to make my breaks."

That is what I've been trying to do for the last 20 years, make my break whether it is in books, radio, or television. A lot of my success is the direct result of the people who have been a blessing in my life who have encouraged me, inspired me, given me a role model of excellence, helped me along the way, or given me advice and direction.

Monica: That leads me to my next question. When you were trying to find your niche, who supported you? Who cheered you on?

Willie: I direct a good portion of my success to the National Speakers Association. I joined the National Speakers Association and they encouraged me. Not just as a community but individually. They gave me insight, advice, and direction. I've had numerous mentors.

Monica: Who are some of your mentors?

Willie: Les Brown, Zig Ziglar, Brian Tracy, and W. Mitchell have all been good friends and mentors. Rosita Perez, the speaker who passed away a couple of years ago, was like my godmother in the speaking arena. Harvey Mackay and Dennis Kimbrough helped me with writing books and becoming an author. A lot of people over the years helped me in radio, including Cathy Hughes. I've still got a lot of learning to do. Moving into television is my next big goal. Of course, there will be some people that I will learn from on that path.

Monica: Would you say that there is a common denominator that kept you focused when you were trying to turn your life around? What allows you to stay grounded through all of your extraordinary success today?

Willie: Without question, faith is the common denominator. It is He who does the work through me. I have tried it without God in my life and tried it with God in my life, and I had so much more success when I decided to trust God through the process. My success is built directly on my faith.

Monica: What does success mean to you?

Willie: Success to me means a constant, ongoing pursuit and achievement of a worthy idea. You make a plan, do it, and you move into that direction. That's success. You might not achieve it quickly but it is the process of moving into that direction.

Monica: It is amazing how many people have unfulfilled dreams. I sometimes hear people say, "You don't dream big enough."

Willie: That's true. Most people don't dream big enough. Anderson said, "If you could realize what you could achieve, you would amaze yourself." Most people settle for smaller dreams, smaller vision, and smaller sights. They have been conditioned since childhood to stop dreaming big.

Monica: What are some things that you are most thankful for?

Willie: I am most thankful for my faith, my family, and my friends. Everything else takes secondary preference.

Monica: Can you leave my readers with a positive thought?

Willie: I always have a last word. When the time comes for me to die, I am going to bounce up out of the box and say that I've got one more thing to say. I tell people that you must wake up and dream big dreams. You must show up and always give your best. You must stand up and become the leader that's within you. You must step up to the plate and swing for the center. And last, but not least, you must think up and make up your mind to win.

Keys to Programming Your Mindset for Ultimate Success

America's Mental Toughness Coach, Dr. Clint Pearman, shares powerful insights on how to reprogram your mind and create a mindset for success. Dr. Pearman has discovered why people don't fully use their God-given talents and why so many of us are not living up to our true potential.

As a high school athlete, he maintained a winning attitude that he garnered from his coaches, his father, and his older brother. After graduating from high school, Pearman spent the next 31 years of his life in the world's premiere leadership and mental toughness training organization—the U.S. Marine Corps. In the Marines, he observed the methodology used to prepare young soldiers to become some of the mentally toughest people in the world who excel under adverse conditions and in extreme environments.

As the founder of Copenology, an organization exploring the brain science of optimum human performance, Pearman has applied Copenology principles in a variety of fields, ranging from recruiting for the Marines to Navy sailors trying to lose weight. He has also provided personal relationship coaching and uses the knowledge that he obtained through education and research to train sales teams at major corporations. He motivates individuals to realize their capabilities and to view obstacles as opportunities.

He is the founder and chief researcher of the North American Center for Optimum Performance Enabling Neuroscience (NACOPEN), a research and development company focused on identifying and synthesizing cutting-edge brain science research.

The editor-in-chief of *Exceptional People Magazine* was delighted to have Pearman share key elements of the methods he uses to help people reach their potential and achieve success.

Monica: You are often referred to as "America's Mental Toughness Coach." How did you earn that title?

Clint: I joined the Marines right after high school. I spent 18 years on active duty and went into the Reserves after I was done with my service. While in the Reserves, I noticed that the Marines develop people in a special way. The Marine Corps accepts a person at ages 17, 18, or 19, right out of high school, or at ages 26 or 27, right out of college. They give them basic training and place them in the world's most dangerous, stressful, and challenging conditions. The Marine Corps expects them to succeed and excel in this environment.

When I was in the Reserves, I began observing and studying this technique. I wanted to know what the Marine Corps does that allows them to expect people to excel in this type of situation when most people would not survive. Over the next ten years, while in the Reserves, I did what I call an informal investigation or an informal study of the Marine Corps.

My last two years I was mobilized and put on active duty for the global war on terrorism. I put in for retirement in 2004. It was denied, and I was mobilized, which gave me almost 18 months of intense research. At the end of those two years, I figured out what the Marine Corps was doing.

I realized it was essentially developing mental toughness in its Marines. That allowed them to use their minds and brains to focus on each step of an individual goal until it was completed. I realized anyone could accomplish anything if they learned how to focus on each step of a single goal until it was completed. I started teaching this during my last 12 months on active duty when I realized that these things apply to human performance.

Monica: What has serving in the Marines for 30 years taught you about life and how to survive during the most trying times?

Clint: I've learned lots of things, but that last ten years while I was in the Reserves. Then the last two years on active duty is where I formulated the concept of the mental toughness paradigm. I show people how to use their minds and brains to live up to their potential and avoid underachievement. I can share the three most powerful things I learned about achieving success during my 31 years in the Marines.

The first is *mental programming*. Some people might call it brainwashing, but I like to say if you're being brainwashed to learn how to live up to your potential, that's a fantastic form of brainwashing. From the day you enter into boot camp, the Marine Corps begins transforming you, and it begins with changing the way you think, changing your beliefs, and changing your mental paradigms.

Next, the Marine Corps conditions your body for optimum performance. They put you through intensive physical training from the beginning and help you maintain that form until you retire. In order to live up to your potential, your body has to be able to perform what your mind wants it to do.

The third most powerful thing I learned was, once your mind is programmed properly and your body is conditioned to produce what your mind wants it to do, the only thing left to do is to figure out a way to automate that behavior. That essentially involves developing goals. We are always goal driven in the Marine Corps. We always have goals and plans that tell us what to do. If the first part of the plan doesn't work, it's OK because there's always a back-up plan.

Monica: You are also a success coach. What methods do you employ to have people reach their true potential?

Clint: One of the main reasons people hire coaches is that they have a goal that they're trying to achieve and they want help. Through my coaching philosophy, I apply those same three principles of mental programming, physical conditioning, and goal setting. Once your mind is programmed, you can accomplish any goal you set.

After developing a mindset, you need physical conditioning. You don't need world-class Olympic conditioning.

Let's say you have a 9-5 job and you're trying to build a business on the side. That's going to require a lot of energy and endurance. What if you're not physically conditioned to work your 9-5 job and come home to build your business?

We say in the success arena, "Your 9-5 job is just the starting point for building your future because your future begins after your 9-5 job ends. That means you may need to be in better physical condition to build a business than you need to work your 9-5 job because now you're putting in double the hours. Believe it or not many people never live up to their potential because they're physically incapable of everything that's required. You hear people say, "I'm tired." Well, that's an example of not being physically ready.

Once your mind is right and your body is right, you simply need the plan. I sometimes refer to that as the GPS. Turn on your GPS, put in the program, and take off. Your mind and body will automatically steer you in the direction of your goals and plans when they're physically and mentally programmed.

Monica: I have often observed that people are not motivated to accomplish their dreams and goals. Why do you think some people are self-motivated and others are not?

Clint: When we're born, we are totally dependent on someone to take care of us. We're incapable of doing anything on our own, but we eventually grow to be codependent. Somewhere around six years old, we become codependent, we can do things on our own, but we still need our parents to continue our development.

After codependence, around 13 or 14 years of age, we begin observing the actions of the adults and we start what I call independence. It's at that independence stage where a lot of people make the mistake of believing independence is the final stage. They watch adults and the older people in their lives function in what they view as independence, and they think, "That's what I want to do." You hear it often from children and teenagers. They say, "I can't wait to get out on my own." What they're referring to is the independent stage of life. We fail to progress when we stop at independence. We think, "Now I'm out on my own. I graduated from high school or college. I have my own job. I have my own car. I have my own house." Independence is not the final stage.

People become stagnant in the independent stage, and they never reach their full potential simply because they fail to realize the fourth stage of human optimum performance is interdependence. Interdependence is that stage where you learn to work with others. That is when your life begins to flourish.

Once a person is in the interdependent stage, this is where success really takes hold. When you're not motivated, it's generally because your mindset is not programmed properly to do what you want to do. There are four components that involve motivation. You can become motivated from external sources, watching a motivational movie, listening to a motivational speaker, or reading a motivational book.

All of those things will motivate you temporarily, but the goal is to become inspired to go to the next level of motivation. In order to become inspired, there are four factors. One, you need a vision of what you are trying to accomplish. Next, after you have the vision, you need to make a concrete, solid decision to accomplish it. It's amazing how many people have a vision of what they want to achieve, but they never make a decision to accomplish it. Your decision has to involve being committed, no matter how long it takes. The third component is to believe that you can achieve your goal. You have to learn how to engineer that belief. The fourth and final component is to develop a passion for what you want to accomplish. When you develop these four components, motivation is not an issue.

Monica: You have a passion for exploring the depths of brain science. Why are you intrigued by the subject?

Clint: With a psychology background and my coaching and performance development, all my training was done through what I knew about psychology. Six years ago, I started reading research about the Decade of the Brain. In the mid-80s, scientists at the National Institutes of Science and Health began lobbying Congress for funding. They believed that they were on the verge of unbelievable breakthroughs.

Already being in the environment of succeeding and having a background in psychology, I was able to visualize this research and see how it could be synthesized and redeveloped into human performance. That's what motivated me to pursue the subject of brain science. I became aware of the enormous amount of research that could be applied to determine what happens when we learn to live up to our potential. I found there was an enormous amount of research in this area. I called it Copenology. Essentially, Copenology is brain research that can be applied to human performance.

Monica: You are the chief researcher and founder of NACOPEN, the North American Center for Optimum Performance Enabling Neuroscience. What is its purpose?

Clint: When I began noticing all of the research coming out of the Decade of the Brain, I realized it's going to take some effort to continue this research and convert it into something that people can use. NACOPEN Research is the research company that takes brain science research, synthesizes it, and converts it into Copenology, which is the new brain science for success. It's put into layman's terms. I take that brain science research and show how it applies to things such as goal-setting, time management, focus, confidence, commitment—those success modalities.

Monica: Over the years I have realized that we can be great procrastinators. Is there a connection between procrastination and brain science?

Clint: Procrastination is one of the most important solutions that Copenology can solve. When you think about the science of Copenology, it is ideal for solving a person's procrastination problems because it changes the mindset. I often tell people there is no such thing as procrastination. It's a mindset. When we think of procrastination, what we're really thinking of is priorities. We don't procrastinate; we simply don't do what we want to do. We do what our mind is programmed to tell us to do.

For example, if you have a goal to lose weight and you procrastinate about going to the gym, what you're really doing is prioritizing something else. If we can program your mind and brain to do what you want to do, you won't procrastinate anymore. That's what Copenology is all about. When you ask if there's a tie between procrastination and brain science, there is a direct connection. Procrastination is all about how your mind is set up. Brain science can teach you how to reprogram your mind.

Monica: For many years you have helped corporate America improve productivity and develop teams that are motivated to achieve excellence. How do you apply your mental toughness methodology to the corporate arena? What do you find most rewarding when you teach corporate America about excellence?

Clint: The first thing you should understand when you ask that question is our brains are involved in everything we do. When you learn how to manage your brain, you can control almost everything. One of the major challenges in corporate America is we're learning how to manage behavior, functions, and processes which are all controlled or directed by our brains.

But if our brains are not functioning properly, you can't expect those other processes to function properly. I teach people how to develop the power of their brain to do the things they need to do.

Let's take a company that has a sales force. We know sales are 90% mental. Unless your salespeople are taught to develop mental power, they will never perform up to their potential because they lack mental toughness. Once you develop mental toughness, you no longer see obstacles. They're simply viewed as something you need to overcome.

Another example might be the customer service department. Until your customer service people understand how to develop a mental program so that they see their customers in the right light, they'll never learn to provide exceptional customer service.

Monica: I've noticed that when someone asks you how you're doing, you always say, "Fantastic." How do you put yourself in a fantastic frame of mind?

Clint: Science is teaching us and telling us that the mind-body connection is unbelievably important to our health and well-being. In other words, how we think, how we use our minds is important. In fact, more than 90 percent of the illnesses we suffer from today have a mental mindset component which is primarily stress-related.

I always respond with "fantastic" because I understand how important our minds are to our health, and I want to live a healthy life as long as I possibly can. That begins with controlling how your mind affects your body. Your brain literally affects your body. You can think yourself into being sick or you can think yourself into being healthy.

I tell people you can wake up every day and decide how you want your day to be. When you wake up, you literally choose either consciously or subconsciously how your day is going to be. I wake up every day, and I say, "Lord, thank you for giving me another day. I am going to make this a fantastic day." I don't care what's going on externally. Internally, I am going to have a fantastic day.

First, you have to decide you want to be fantastic when you first wake up and begin the mental process by saying it. It doesn't matter whether you are feeling fantastic at that time. If you begin telling yourself you are fantastic, you will program yourself to believe you are.

Monica: What can you pass on to others about achieving success by using your mental toughness method?

Clint: Your mind and brain controls everything you do. When you learn to control your mind and brain, then you'll live up to your potential.

"Employees are a company's greatest asset—they're your competitive advantage. You want to attract and retain the best; provide them with encouragement, stimulus, and make them feel that they are an integral part of the company's mission."

Anne M. Mulcahy

Section 10

Other Success Stories

Competitive Analysis and Research: A Necessity for a Good Business Foundation

Innovative entrepreneur Nicko Williamson, CEO of Climatecars, shares his story about starting a new company that is also helping to improve his environment.

London's Green Entrepreneur Achieves Success with Climatecars

How many of us can say that at age 22 we wanted to become an entrepreneur? Londoner Nicko Williamson did just that. While attending Marlborough College, he saw himself becoming his own boss. But, more important, he wanted to make a significant contribution to his country's environment.

Nicko has begun to see the fruits of his labor after three years of hard work to begin his company, Climatecars. Not only is he fulfilling his dream as an entrepreneur and contributing to changing London's environment, but Nicko's entrepreneurial endeavor has become an asset to London's economy. He employs more than 60 employees. In today's world that's a major feat, especially for the 27-year-old entrepreneur extraordinaire.

Nicko's dream behind Climatecars was to introduce a vehicle that would have lower levels of emissions, thereby helping to create a greener environment. He is succeeding. His goal is to become the first company to provide a 100% emission-free taxi service.

Climatecars has changed the tone of London's taxicab industry. Nicko saw a need and quickly began to fill it. As the top green cab company, Nicko wanted to ensure that his customers would not sacrifice comfort and convenience. As a matter of fact, Climatecars offers enhanced customer service from the time that the customers are picked up until they arrive at their destinations.

Let's take an interesting trip into Nicko's entrepreneurial dream as he shares his experience with *Exceptional People Magazine*.

Monica: Tell me about yourself in terms of growing up and what life was like in your high school years.

Nicko: I went to a boarding school called Marlborough College in Wiltshire. At age 18, I went to Bristol University and studied Modern History, which, of course, is a bit unrelated to what I'm doing now. That was my main degree when I was there.

I was always thinking about what I was going to be doing while my friends were applying to become investment bankers and entering other professions. I wanted to start my own business.

While I was at Bristol, I had the idea for Climatecars. It started during my last year at the university while I was writing my dissertation. I was scribbling down ideas about Climatecars, and it progressed to the point where I began writing a business plan.

Upon leaving Bristol University I began to focus on Climatecars. It took me a year after leaving Bristol to start the company in 2006.

Monica: What was your vision behind starting Climatecars?

Nicko: My vision was an eco-friendly taxi company. I could see that everybody was using taxis; taxis are incredibly popular in London. I thought, "Why not make this green?" I couldn't see a reason why it couldn't be green.

I started looking at gas conversion as my first idea. I was going to convert them to run on liquefied petroleum gas (LPG), which has a lower emission than petrol or diesel. Then, I decided that really wasn't the way because I couldn't get it to work or make the emissions savings stack up. About that time the new generation of Toyota Prius came out and it was the obvious thing to use.

We didn't have to convert the Toyota Prius. If you compare a Prius to a standard black taxi, which are what most people use to get around town, the emissions on the new model Prius is around 89 grams per kilometer. The black cab is around 230 grams per kilometer at the low end and 270 grams per kilometer at the high end. The savings are vast and there's no difficulty in doing it. We didn't have to charge more for our service. Although there is no lower level of service, I wanted to create something that was better than our competitors.

All of our cars have leather seats and are stocked with magazines and an environmentally friendly branded bottle of water. Each car is driven by a smart driver who delivers great service. I want to be the car company that people or companies will feel good about themselves as they care about the environment.

Monica: I would imagine that you had to acquire funding. How were you able to get the funding and what challenges, if any, did you encounter?

Nicko: When I left the university, I was 22 years old. I had never run a business and had never worked for anybody although I had participated in some internships. I didn't have a lot of credible experience behind me. I knew a lot of entrepreneurs, and I sought a lot of advice. One of them told me to go work for a taxi company in London, pick apart the business, and build myself a bible on how to operate this type of business.

So, at age 22, I went off and did that. I came to understand the process. I went back to the entrepreneur, and he was quite surprised that I did it. He began advising and mentoring me. By this time, I was in a good position. I had a business plan and I had also attended London Business School, which is the business equivalent of Harvard or Yale in the United States.

I approached the business school with the idea and asked for help. They put two MBA students on it, and we actually entered a business planning competition. The Global Social Venture Competition is for businesses with an environmental or social impact. These two individuals were able to help me with the numbers, and I was able to build a solid, robust business plan.

Then I approached a network of people who I knew had funds they may want to invest. I explained that I was trying to raise £200,000 to start the business. A number of them said yes.

I submitted the plan and it's amazing. The first person that I sent my business plan to contacted me and said he would give me £50,000. Another person came along and gave me £25,000 and another gave £20,000. I was over halfway there and suddenly the rest of it kind of fell into place. I managed to get a few relatives to contribute as well.

It was all equity funding where I sold 30% of the company back in 2007. That allowed me to be adequately capitalized. I also leased vehicles, and that gave me capital that I needed to start.

Monica: When you were learning how to run a business by working for a rival taxi company, how long did that process take?

Nicko: About three months. I was young and impatient. I literally crawled all over the business, spoke to everybody, and tried to identify their weaknesses. I could have spent more time, and I probably should have spent more time to be honest. I probably would have avoided some mistakes. It wasn't a very well-run business, so I didn't want to shape my business based on that business. I just wanted to learn from their mistakes and understand the market.

I had a timeframe in my head that I wanted to get this done within a year from leaving the university. It was just before Christmas that I left the company. I allowed myself a couple of months to raise cash, get an office, and hire people. It was a bit hurried, but I feel when you have momentum you need to push on with it.

Monica: What makes your eco-friendly car different?

Nicko: The differentiating factor with us is that we offer a really great service with lots of extras and added value beyond what other companies offer. We offer more of a corporate car service than a normal taxi service at a very competitive price. It's not just the eco-friendly side. It's the little things. When you get picked up from the airport, there's a cold bottle of water waiting for you and a driver meeting you in a suit that looks smart and will help you with your bags. It comes down to great service. It's the core of our business.

Monica: Your goal is to combine ecology, economy, and innovation to provide the most comfortable service.

Nicko: That was one of our initial goals. We're now working on new innovations. I've hired a new operations director this year who has taken on the day-to-day operations which has freed up a lot of time to allow me to focus on strategy. I'm now looking at the next stage of the business. Now, I'm focusing on running a fleet of totally electric cars and combining that range by offering hybrid vehicles. We're going to be using the U.K. version of the Chevy Volt and Rena. Both companies are coming out with a variety of electric vehicles as early as next year. By this time next year, we'll have a much better range of vehicles with lower emissions and a more comprehensive range of services while still striving to be the greenest taxi company around.

Monica: Who are your customers or clients?

Nicko: We primarily serve corporate clients. Ninety percent of our revenue comes from business customers, ranging from one very large U.S. investment bank to Unilever to radio stations to ad agencies. We have a very diverse client base. My goal has been to spread our clients as widely as possible. At the same, we ensure that we don't have too many clients taking up too much of our turnover. Our largest clients are no more than 15 to 20% turnover. That gives us stability so that if we were to lose a client, we won't bust.

Monica: Your service is becoming a luxury taxi service?

Nicko: I wouldn't use the word luxury because I don't want people to be put off by price. We are very cost-sensitive and we offer services at a good value price. It's no more expensive than any of our competitors. It's actually often cheaper than the black cab by about two miles. We offer high-quality car service. We have a lot of cash and credit card customers. If you're ever in London and you want to book one of our cars, you can ring us up 24 hours a day or book online. Anybody can book our cars.

Monica: The average person can use your service?

Nicko: Yes, they can call anytime, 24 hours a day, 365 days a year.

Monica: Your vision is to provide first-class service. Your customer service has several components. I'll outline a few of them for you to expand on. The first one is reliability. How do you provide reliability to your customers?

Nicko: We use a lot of technology. We heavily invested in a very good software and hardware system for our vehicle tracking. All of our vehicles are dispatched through our computer system. The jobs are sent to the drivers through a PDA, and we can see exactly where the driver is. If the customer is running late, we can change things around quickly. We are able to monitor every part of the process to ensure that we are able to provide reliable service.

Monica: What value do you bring to your customers?

Nicko: We give great service at the right price and at the lowest possible emissions you can get for this type of service. We're not providing limo service. We are delivering a very comfortable service that's going to show up to get you to your destination on time.

Monica: What about comfort?

Nicko: We offer leather seats, mineral water, clean cars, and drivers who will turn the air conditioning or heat to whatever temperature you want. It's all about comfort and service. People who decide to use us do so because of our green credentials.

Monica: How has Climatecars impacted the economy in London? Have you been able to measure that success?

Nicko: We have not been able to measure the company's success in relation to the London economy as a whole, but we've grown tremendously. We've been going for four years and last year we did £2.2 million of turnover. It's been growing really nicely and we're planning on doing over £3 million of turnover next year. Assuming things continue to go well, I think it's having a very positive effect on the economy in London.

Monica: Absolutely. You're putting people to work.

Nicko: We have over 60 drivers as well as an office staff. It's becoming a big business but we're scaling it up. We're not going to continue to do the same thing. We're going to keep innovating. There will be other services that are complementary to this one.

Monica: Your aim is to be the first zero emissions car service. How far are you from reaching that goal?

Nicko: We're getting quite close. We've got electric vehicles coming early next year. These cars will generally be zero emissions. There's always the challenge of where to get our electricity. There's a lack of renewable electricity in the U.K., which is a bit of a problem. But we will be providing cars that do not emit any CO_2 at all when they're driving around town. They'll be purely electric.

Within a year, part of our fleet will be at that point. We're a ways off from being able to offer purely electric vehicles for the whole fleet because we need to make some longer distance trips. The issue with electric vehicles is range. The ones we're using are going to have a 100-mile range. Therefore, we're only going to be able to have a portion of our fleet solely electric. The remainder will be range-extending hybrids and other new technology.

Monica: To what do you attribute the success of your company?

Nicko: A lot of hard work and pretty good marketing. It's a solid idea and decent product. We've gone into an existing market and tweaked the product. It's better, different, and interesting. I think that's where the success comes from. We're not trying to invent something new and revolutionary. Our product allows us to enter a market and receive decent market share fairly quickly because people need this service. We're very proud of our brand.

Monica: From a business standpoint what are some important lessons you've learned since starting the company?

Nicko: The first is cash flow. Taxies are a very cash-intensive business. We've been profitable for quite a while now, but in the beginning, it was very tough. It's difficult to run the business when you're not making money or when several companies are delaying their payment terms. One of the key things I've learned is managing cash.

You also have to keep innovating. You have to make sure you have a good sales team and a good story that's well marketed. I started doing all the sales myself. Now, we have two people who do the sales and marketing for us. That's very important.

Also, make sure you have a very good numbers person. We're lucky to have a helpful finance director who stays on top of the key metrics of the business. If you're going to run anything operational, you absolutely need to know every little number that's driving different areas of the business.

Monica: One of the main keys to operating a successful business is a solid marketing plan and team.

Nicko: We use public relations to generate press. Our cars are branded subtlety. We also do e-campaigns and cold calling. We're not re-inventing the wheel. We're doing a lot of search engine optimization and other related things.

Monica: Within a short period of time your company has grown tremendously.

Nicko: Yes, thankfully. We've got to keep it going now.

Monica: What advice can you give other young entrepreneurs about starting a business?

Nicko: I would say one of the key things is assembling a good team. I was lucky with my London Business School associates and a few other people I involved in the business. Although I was running it myself, I was able to pick up the phone and get advice and help from them. Without it, the business wouldn't be where it is today.

Make sure to research any new business you are thinking about. Many people dive into things without really understanding the market, the players, and the competitors. I did a lot of competitive analysis before I started. I knew exactly what I was up against and what other companies were charging. I researched everything about the car and taxi market in London. Make sure the planning process is well done. If you miss something, the business can be completely and fundamentally flawed.

Monica: Looking back on everything that you've done so far, is there anything that you would do differently?

Nicko: It's very easy to say that in hindsight. I would probably say staffing. We had many difficulties with early members of the staff. I probably would have spent more money on recruitment rather than advertising. It took a while to assemble the right team, but it's really difficult to say how we would have done it. The right people are generally attracted to some form of success, but when you're starting a business from scratch, you have no success or track record. So it is not easy to get the right people involved in the business. We've made many mistakes and have learned from all of them. It's part of the learning process. It's managing while learning. If you've got the determination to make it succeed, it's possible.

Monica: Any last words?

Nicko: I really think entrepreneurs are going to rebuild the world economy. With a little determination, hard work, and building good teams, anything is possible.

Living Your Passion

Creative entrepreneur Ellen Banks, President of Transformational Tees, shares her story on why she decided to quit her job and take control of her life.

Are You Living Your Passion? Take a Leap of Faith!

Have you ever had a dream? A vision of doing something you love or something that would transform your life and maybe the lives of others? Eight years after reflecting on her ideas and dreams, Ellen Banks found a pathway to entrepreneurial freedom.

One afternoon, Ellen made a split-second decision to quit her job. It wasn't that she didn't have a successful career as a business woman. But she wanted her life to be more fulfilling. She wanted something different. Ellen envisioned a business that would keep her focused on her goals while helping others to focus on their paths to personal transformation. She even came up with a name for her company—Transformation Tees.

An Amsterdam native, Ellen and her family moved to the United States in the early 1960s. She graduated from Centenary College after dedicating herself to attending night classes for 10 years. Her deep passion and contributions to higher education garnered her the prestigious Van Winkle award in 2000. She was a founding member of the President's Circle and a member of the Capital Campaign Steering Committee.

Ten years ago, Ellen never would have thought that she could impact so many lives. But one afternoon, she got an idea that would eventually change her life as well as the lives of her family and others.

Many of us often have moments of enlightenment, but we tend to let them fade away. We often have goals and dreams, but life challenges can deter or require us to put our dreams on hold. Even though you can't fulfill your dream at a given time and place, it doesn't mean you give up.

Raising a family and working as a career woman temporarily took precedence over Ellen's vision, but she never gave up. She says, "The whispers never stopped." When you have a true passion for something, it will stay with you until you decide to do something about it.

"I was on the fast track in my career," Ellen said. "After thinking about the idea, it went into the filing cabinet for a while."

Eight years after she first had her idea, it became reality. Transformation Tees was born. Ellen not only transformed her life but the lives of many others.

Ellen says, "I believe we are given information for a reason. As with many inspirations we have in life, we are only vehicles to getting certain things accomplished, especially if the end result is positive for others."

How many of you have a dream you'd like to fulfill, but for one reason or another, haven't done anything about it? Do the realities of life seem to get in the way? Ellen answered this question and more during an interview with *Exceptional People Magazine*.

Monica: What was the moment you experienced that altered your life and your view of life?

Ellen: We lived in New Jersey, and my commute to Manhattan was awful and very challenging. I was sitting on a bus in traffic for two hours. There was always something happening. We had another tanker turn over and I thought, "This is a waste of life."

I started thinking about what else I could do. It was a huge leap to go from working on Park Avenue to starting a clothing company, but I said, "That's it."

I got off at the exit, went to the Staples store, bought a flip chart, and wrote Transformation Tees on it. We had an old barn that we used for our offices. It was full of hay and I just hung the sign there. I said, "This is where I want to be, and this is what I'm going to do."

My husband said to me, "I think we need to call a psychiatrist." It was crazy.

My daughter said, "Mom, you know I'm going to college next year. What are you doing?"

I said. "This feels right and if I don't do it now, I won't do it."

I liked the idea of leaving my career on a high note. Corporate America was so good to me. It gave me the tools and knowledge that I needed to start this company. After 30 years, I decided to retire. I told them, "You could pay me a million dollars next year, but it doesn't matter. It's not about the money."

I was always trying to fit my life into my work. Now I fit my work into my life. It's a big change. In almost 30 years I had never had two weeks of vacation in a row. I was always so busy. When you're on vacation, they're always calling you on the beach. You have to have your laptop with you. It's like being on a crazy treadmill.

Monica: You went from corporate America to starting your own business. Did you feel you had the funds to really get the business going?

Ellen: I decided to take a leap of faith. I approached the bank about two years ago. I gave my business plan to a friend in banking and I said, "If you have faith in my company to the point that you'd want to invest in it, then I know I'll be OK." He took me on as a customer, and I began working with an investor.

I built the company as if I were building an Aetna or General Electric. I got good lawyers, and I trademarked everything the right way so that I would not feel vulnerable. Today, we have two employees. Tomorrow, I'm ready to have 100 employees. It took me about six months to build everything.

Transformation Tees, LLC, officially launched on June 21, 2007 at "Solstice in Times Square." We were the official tee shirt sponsor of the annual Times Square Alliance/Yoga Journal event.

Monica: What was the defining moment that made you finally decide to quit your job and start your business?

Ellen: The tremendous strain of commuting. Getting home at 8:00 p.m. each night and starting dinner so late in the evening. Realizing that my child would be moving away to college in a year. I thought, "I never really spent an entire summer with her. I need to spend time with her before she grows up and leaves the nest." That is what got the ball rolling.

Monica: What do you find most rewarding about being in business for yourself?

Ellen: Having total control of my time and my ideas. When you work in a corporation, you have to be a routine player quite often. You have great ideas and they don't get picked up or you don't get the credit for them. You make a lot of money for other people. When you are in business for yourself, it's up to you whether you make it or break it. I also enjoy being able to have a passion about something and expressing it.

Monica: How has Transformation Tees transformed your life?

Ellen: Oh, boy! It's given me lots of lessons. Good ones and bad ones. I feel Transformation Tees and I are on this journey together. I will often pull out everything and say, "Here's where we were a year ago." With every start of a business you will have your challenges, ups and downs, good periods and slow periods.

You have to stay motivated, and you have to stay true to the end goal. I will often pull out pictures and marketing material to remind myself how far I've come. It really challenges you. If I say, "I think I have done everything I possibly can," the next day another idea comes along. I've learned from people in various departments when I was working in corporate America. Now I am those departments. It was wonderful to learn all of that.

Monica: What advice or inspiration can you give other women about following their dreams?

Ellen: I would say just do it, but do it in a very careful way. If you're not in the position to do what I did or you can't do it part-time, don't give up your dream. Work in your day job and start to do the research. Build the foundation in your free time and get yourself in a position where you feel like you can make that move.

Do lots of research. See what else is out there. Make sure you know your target market. You may have a great idea, but no one else out there thinks it's a great idea. You don't want to risk putting a lot of capital into building something when there really is no market for it.

Monica: What is the overall message you want to get across through your t-shirts?

Ellen: Believe in the power of yourself and that strength comes from within. Through the power of visualization, you can stay focused on something. People are using visualization as a tool to remind themselves that they are strong and they can do it, whatever their "it" is.

Monica: What were some things that you learned in the process of quitting your job and starting a business? You had no experience in developing a product. How did you prepare yourself for this type of business?

Ellen: I surrounded myself with experts. My career was in marketing, sales, and claims, so I had no experience in manufacturing clothing. But I knew experts in that field, and I used them as consultants to help launch my business. I also did a lot of homework. We lived very close to Centenary College, and I asked one of the professors in the fashion department to teach me about materials. You have to surround yourself with good people. You need expert people you can trust and will have your back. You also have to educate yourself so that you know you're not being led down the wrong road.

Monica: Where do you see your vision in the next three years?

Ellen: I want the company to be very profitable and all the capitalization loans to be paid in full. We're now in a position where we can really expand the product. We now have a wonderful jewelry line made from very natural gemstones with healing properties. I'd like to see that grow. In ten years, I'd like to do my manufacturing in one of the old factories or buildings in town and help revitalize my town in New Jersey. My goal is to grow in such a way that we are in a financial position to do that.

Monica: What has been your overall experience in moving from your regular job to going into business for yourself? What has that meant to you and how has it given you a different view on life?

Ellen: It's been a wonderfully challenging, enlightening, and scary experience. It has allowed me to get my life back a different way. It has opened my eyes to the world around me that I didn't see before. It has allowed me to really challenge myself.

Monica: Despite those challenges and the scary times that you experienced, would you still encourage others to follow their dreams?

Ellen: Absolutely. As we get older, we see the horrors around us—young people dying and car accidents. Think of it this way. If you knew that you were going to close your eyes tomorrow and God calls you, would you say "That's OK because I'm really happy with how I have lived my life?" Or would you say, "Darn! I wish I was doing what I always dreamed of doing." Have you been living your passion? Have you been living your dream? If not, get busy doing that. It's never too late to start.

From Rags to Riches

International fragrance designer Geir Ness, President of Laila, shares his experience of developing a new product and the creative strategy he used to get it onto the market. Use his creative idea as an example to think of ways to open new doors for your business.

The Sweet Smell of Norway, Part I

Geir Ness has the ability to easily draw people into a real conversation and a personality that lights up a room. But his road to success was not straightforward. Growing up in Norway with a father who was a ski instructor, Geir learned to ski before he could walk. He became very involved in other outdoor sports, but playing sports wasn't his only passion. His interest in acting and Hollywood was heightened by viewing photos of Hollywood actors that his mom showed him.

He enjoyed play acting with his friends. He continued to act as a young adult and his coach encouraged him to come to America to become more involved in acting. He was delighted that his instructor believed in him.

Geir soon set his sights on Los Angeles, California, where he began studying acting on a student loan. Upon arriving, he quickly realized what a challenge he would have because he had little money and spoke very little English. How did he manage in fast-paced LA? After purchasing a car for $600 and renting a modest apartment, his next challenge was learning to speak English. He began watching television and reading newspapers to learn English. This helped him greatly as he continued acting. It was a challenge, but it taught him not to give up, no matter how tough the situation may seem.

Realizing he had to supplement his income, Geir accepted a job offered by a friend to become a fragrance model. He had no idea what that meant. His magnetic personality drew people to him and they would often ask where he was from and if Norway had perfumers. That was the beginning of Geir's interest in learning more about the perfume business.

Geir began researching combinations of fragrances that would reflect the beauty and essence of Norway, something light and fresh. A friend was kind enough to lend him money to help him start his business. While developing and perfecting fragrances, he would often seek the opinion of others. He believed that the best way to perfect his product would be to obtain the opinion of potential customers.

Several years later, he introduced, Laila and Geir, his personal line of perfumes and colognes. Since the process of developing Laila took five years from conception to reality, Geir learned a lot about himself during that time.

After years of development and testing, he had 1,000 bottles of Laila sitting in his apartment. His reaction was, "What am I going to do now? Where do I start?"

Reality set in. Geir had no experience selling a fragrance line and his money had run out. He immediately began to contact department stores and quickly found out that it was going to be an uphill battle. He was not a celebrity and he had no experience in fragrance distribution. Undeterred by the challenge, he began to think of ways to market his fragrances. He contacted a major department store. Although they liked the product, he was told that he would never be successful without money to distribute and market it. Geir challenged the store to order 100 bottles. If they did not sell, he would take them back after three months. It took six months to get a meeting with store officials. They accepted the offer.

Geir was scheduled to appear at the department store the day before Mother's Day. Not knowing anything about the business, Geir's creative thinking kicked in and he decided to market himself. He went to a garage sale and purchased a five-dollar suit and a red carpet. He contacted a photographer friend whose funds were so low that he couldn't afford film for his camera. This didn't stop Geir. When the store opened, the photographer pretended to snap photographs. People began lining up, including celebrities. This was Hollywood. People wanted to know more about this person and what he was selling. Geir began signing autographs and selling perfume. It was an exciting day for him.

As he greeted customers, he felt something biting him on the back, but he continued without a flinch. That day was a successful one for Geir. He sold every bottle of fragrance and had a waiting list of 50 people. Upon returning home after an exciting day, Geir discovered that his suit had fleas in it. He was so poor that he could not afford to have the suit dry cleaned. Still, it had been a glamorous experience for him. His ability to think outside the box created a whole new world of opportunities.

Geir believes that to become successful you have to believe in yourself and your product 110%. You have to be willing to make sacrifices, put in the extra hours, and never let anyone discourage you from accomplishing your goals. He knows how easy it can be to give up, but he chose not to do so.

I have spoken with many entrepreneurs and business people and the advice is always same—be willing to hang in there. Don't give up after a few weeks or even months of trying. Keep focusing on and working toward your goal. Before you know it, when you least expect it, things will begin to happen.

Geir always had a great appreciation for his parents. His mother Laila is his pride and joy. To show his appreciation for her inspiration and encouragement, he secretly copied her signature and placed it on bottles of perfume. He gave his mother her first bottle on Mother's Day. It was one of the best moments of her life to learn that her son cared enough to use her name on his perfume line.

As we chatted, he vividly remembered how his mother used to take him for walks in the mountains. There he would see and smell wild flowers growing in the fields. She has always been supportive of him and his dreams.

Geir's dad was a businessman, and he taught him how to purchase, sell products, and become successful. His dad taught him to trust in himself. He always said to him, "Never hand any part of your business over to someone without some knowledge of what's to be accomplished."

Having developed a potentially successful product, Geir found there was little time to take acting jobs. However, his acting experience was instrumental in helping him meet people and introduce his product line. He's never regretted not continuing to act full time. He continues to use the experience to market his products. Sometimes life has a way of taking you down a beaten path.

Geir believes in a hands-on approach and personal touch when it comes to his customers. He travels over 200 days out of the year to promote his products. He wants his customers to know the person behind the products. To maintain his stamina, Geir exercises regularly and maintains a healthy diet, although it can be difficult when he is traveling.

He also states that having inner happiness and peace is very important to success. Geir's happiness and cheerful spirit are contagious. I knew we were going to have a wonderful conversation as soon as we began to chat. We all experience setbacks and adversities in one form or another, but we should not allow them to adversely affect our ability to think positively.

Geir's products are well known among the stars. His Laila product line has been included in gift bags at various award ceremonies, including the Grammy Awards. Now, he has an extended line of Laila products including perfume, body lotion, deodorant, body bronzer, candles, and many other products. His men's collection also includes a cologne and deodorant.

Throughout his travels, Geir often contributes to charitable causes and takes time to speak on the importance of fitness and good health. He also finds time to share his views on the importance of dedication and being surrounded by positive-thinking people. He encourages people to "focus on the good things you have today." He maintains an upbeat attitude and never-ending patience.

Running a Business During an Economy Downturn

The Sweet Smell of Norway, Part II

Looking great, smelling great, and being a savvy businessman! He's got what it takes! What is "IT"? "IT" is the daring spirit of being in total control of his entrepreneurial destiny, the ability to know when to go against the grain and when to ride the wave. Geir Ness has men and women all over the country smelling, looking, and feeling great. He's helping women feel good about themselves, not only through his products but also through his inspirational presentations.

Geir has gone from cents to scents. He went from making very little money and wearing a five-dollar suit to a multimillion-dollar business. Geir's empire of scents became reality after a customer asked him a simple question over 10 years ago. At the time he was selling perfume in the cosmetics section of a department store. What was the question? It was simple—"Does Norway have its own perfume?" The rest is history. From that one question came a bold idea that has turned into tremendous success. Geir's journey was preceded by years of trials and disappointments, but he made it work.

Over 10 years ago, fragrance designer Geir started his line with Laila, a perfume for women, which he dedicated to his mother on Mother's Day. This was followed by his men's cologne, Geir. All of his fragrances are made from natural ingredients. Geir continues to work with various charities, including the Norwegian Cancer Society and Susan G. Komen for the Cure. He also raises money for abused children.

From time to time, we like to follow-up with entrepreneurs we've previously interviewed to find out what's happening with them and their entrepreneurial endeavors. We interviewed Geir a while ago and decided to check in on him. He has expanded his business to include many other products for men and women. Here's what Geir has been up to lately.

Monica: Has the recession affected your business at all?

Geir: People are not rushing into the department stores right now. What I've been doing is becoming a part of fashion shows or other events at the department stores. You have to be smart and think about where the customers are going and then try to be a part those events. I also have a personal story that I share with customers about how the fragrance Laila began. It's a story that people can relate to.

When I'm at Disney World, I try to place myself where there are lots of potential customers. Recently I was at Nordstrom's in Orange County, and I probably had my best show since I began the business over 10 years ago. You have to work hard but also work smart. By working smart, you think of ways to make your business succeed in this economy. You do it by thinking outside the box.

Monica: What new products are you currently adding to your line?

Geir: You have to know what customers want. I do research to find out what people want related to my line, even in this economy. So I've been working with dermatologists to come up with a facial product that is unique, affordable, and will help people feel good. I'm also developing a new fragrance that I will debut next year. It's exciting. The key to success is sticking with what you know, being happy with it, and making it grow.

I've also been working on television opportunities to help inspire and motivate people to take care of themselves and fulfill their dreams. I have been working with women for the past 10 years in my business. So many of them have dreams, but they can't make them a reality or they don't know how. I've also met women who have been in abusive relationships. They often tell me their stories, and I want to do something for them and make a difference in their lives.

I have a background in health and fitness. I travel over 200 days of the year. It's hard to stay in shape, but if you have a plan and stick with it, it'll work for you.

I also want to do videos and write books.

Monica: How do you explain your longevity in the fragrance business?

Geir: Being consistent, believing in what I do, and believing in my products. You have to believe in yourself, like the people who surround you, and get positive energy from them. If you have people around you who constantly put you down or are always complaining about something, then you become that.

Surround yourself with people who think and act positively even during bad times.

Monica: Looking back, is there anything that you would do differently?

Geir: I said, "Yes" too many times. I went to places with my business that didn't necessarily make money for the company. In the long run, it may have helped get my name out there, but the return on those investments did not pay off. I don't necessarily regret it because I received publicity, but I think I spent too much time on things that didn't help the business grow financially. I learned from that.

Monica: A few years ago, you were practically a one-man business. How many people are currently working for you?

Geir: I have independent contractors who help me with special events. For example, during Christmas I had about 30 to 40 people. I have a person who works at the office, one who does public relations, and one who handles store accounts. The others are independent contractors.

Monica: Do you think you will ever partner with anyone else?

Geir: If the right opportunity comes along.

Monica: What are some of your bestselling products?

Geir: The Laila fragrance, the hand and body cream, and the natural deodorant are some of our bestselling products. The men's cologne, Geir, is also doing very well.

Monica: In the grand scheme of things, how do you want people to feel when they use your products?

Geir: I want them to feel that the products come from love. That's one of the reasons I came up with Laila. I wanted something that reminded me of my mother and my childhood.

Monica: Where do you see the company three years from now?

Geir: The company may become involved with a larger entity that will be able to distribute my products worldwide. I have products in about 200 stores in Europe.

Monica: What makes you most happy?

Geir: Helping people really makes me happy. A couple of years ago, I had a friend who gained weight and had become depressed. I convinced her to come to New York, and I started her on a diet. In one year, she lost almost 100 pounds and became a contestant on "Dancing with the Stars." I see myself making a fitness video, not necessarily for people who want to be in tip-top shape but for those who need to lose weight, want to take care of themselves, and live happy lives.

You can make a difference with your business. You can be a role model to other people and treat people well. You can be nice and kind and still be successful. I want people to look at my product line and my life to see that "this guy" is a kind person and my product line reflects that.

Monica: Any final thoughts?

Geir: Look at yourself as your best friend. How do you treat your best friend? You treat them well. Do the same thing with yourself. Respect yourself and don't put yourself down. Life will be a little easier and you'll find you can make things happen.

The Unexpected Challenges of Running a Business

Entrepreneur extraordinaire Jo Condrill shares the highs and lows of running her own business.

"The greatest achievement was at first and for a time a dream. The oak sleeps in the acorn; the bird waits in the egg; and in the highest vision of the soul a waking angel stirs. Dreams are the seedlings of realities." — James Allen, *As a Man Thinketh*

How I Turned My Dream Business into Reality

Should you own a business? Let me tell you my story.

Life is full of things to do. Some things we must do; others we just want to do. I wanted to start a business of my own. But commuting to work at the Pentagon, working overtime as a civilian, and supervising a staff in Army logistics plans and operations left little time for other things. Whenever I could, I presented seminars based on a six-step process that I developed for getting what you want out of life.

The feedback was very positive. Participants began developing strategies for improving their lives. It was rewarding for me. Guy Kawasaki, author of *The Art of the Start*, said, "Make meaning. Don't focus on making money."

We have an outstanding example in Monica Davis, publisher of *Exceptional People Magazine*.

I squeezed in more productive bits of time to think and plan while I was in the shower or while riding the metro to and from work. The theme that stuck in my mind was "Touching Lives, Making a Positive Difference." I wrote it on purple construction paper and taped the paper high on the wall in the shower stall in my townhouse in Alexandria, VA. It has been the cornerstone of GoalMinds, Inc., a woman-owned small business, during almost 12 years of its existence.

Initially, the focus of GoalMinds was to launch my professional speaking career. My mentor, Dottie Walters, advised that being an author was almost a necessity for becoming a successful speaker. A book serves as a calling card and establishes a person's credibility on a given topic.

An idea for a book occurred to me called *101 Ways to Improve Your Communication Skills Instantly*! I quickly found a coauthor, Bennie Bough, Ph.D., from my master mind group, and within nine months the book was published.

One of my greatest thrills in business has been the sight of that book with my name on the cover and on the shelf of the Fairfax County Library. Now, eleven years later, it has sold thousands of copies and has been translated and sold by publishers in twelve countries around the world.

Take Charge of Your Life: Dare to Pursue Your Dreams is the second edition of *A Millennium Primer: Take Charge of Your Life*, which is my second book. This book provides the steps to success that is the basis for my company GoalMinds. I've presented seminars from Manhattan to San Diego on this topic. Based on the feedback from participants, "Touching Lives, Making a Positive Difference" is working!

At a very successful book signing in El Paso, Texas, one woman who lingered long after the mini-seminar said, "My family is waiting in the car for me, but I don't want to leave."

One victim of spousal abuse said, "This book literally saved my life."

The third book, *From Book Signing to Best Seller: An Insider's Guide to Conducting a Successful Low-Cost Book Signing Tour*, came from my experiences with book signings and tours. These experiences included a signing at the Barnes and Noble store on Fifth Avenue in New York City and a 12-city tour in the southwestern U.S.

As the speaking and seminar business was taking shape, government business opportunities came to my attention. When I attempted to apply for these opportunities, I received the advice to get on a government multiple-award schedule. Someone suggested the Management Organizational and Business Improvement Services (MOBIS) schedule based on my resume. Submitting an offer was a huge learning experience for me. It took a year and many hours of work, but on March 31, 2003, the General Services Administration (GSA) awarded GoalMinds a five-year contract for management consulting, meeting facilitation, and training. GSA extended the contract five more years to 2013. I count this contract among my successes.

Along the way, GoalMinds and I have received recognition. In 2007, the Ford Motor Company and the Greater San Antonio Chamber of Commerce recognized me as an outstanding businesswoman with a "WOW" award. The U.S. Department of Commerce Commercial Service presented GoalMinds with an Export Achievement Certificate for accomplishments in the global marketplace. In 2003, *Real Simple* magazine featured me as the "Wise Woman" in its June/July issue. In 2005, I received a Toastmasters International Presidential Citation.

One of my greatest challenges has been relocating GoalMinds from Los Angeles to San Antonio in January 2005. First, when callers reached my telephone number in LA, the recording simply stated that the phone had been disconnected! It sounded like GoalMinds had gone out of business. I didn't know until a client diligently checked my web page, called, and told me of the message.

I provided a forwarding number when I left LA. The phone company attempted to correct the situation and put a different message on the line. That message gave the new phone number as the old one that had just been disconnected! They failed to see their error, despite several phone calls from me.

Prior to the move, I attempted to make the mail transition a smooth one. I contracted for a commercial mailbox in a national chain store and sent the new address to all my contacts. Within three months, that mailbox franchise went bankrupt and closed.

The U.S. Post Office would only forward mail to the owner of the bankrupt company and he was nowhere to be found. GoalMinds' mail went into oblivion while I notified everyone of another change of address.

Through these challenges, I learned that unless it is absolutely necessary, do not relocate your business! Here are some other things I learned that might help you get started in a business of your own.

- **It takes money to make money.** Potential customers and clients expect us to be competitive with existing businesses. At the very least, you will need professional business cards. This is your door opener, so don't skimp on your cards. A cheap introduction will leave a lasting impression.

  How much money will you need? That depends on the type of business you are going to form. You may have to ask a friend or relative for a loan, use your credit cards as I did, or save up until you have your own money to invest in your business idea. Do it with a positive mental attitude. Don't begrudge the expense. Accept it as "Just the way it is in business."

- **Be reliable.** If you say you are going to do something, do it! Even if you have to give up tickets to the best concert of the season! Your word is your bond.

- **Be magnanimous.** Rise above pettiness. Give more than is required. Ever hear of the baker's dozen? That's when the baker puts in an extra donut with the dozen you paid for. Imitate that example and give more than is expected.

- **Give it all you've got!** Once you have made a decision, believe in yourself. Don't hold back. Have a mentor, a coach, or at least a buddy that you can call to tell of your successes or share a disappointment. Maintain a positive mental attitude.

- **Give back to the community** or your church. There is something about giving that creates a vacuum. Often that vacuum is filled by good things you want in your life. My giving back has taken various avenues. I joined Rotary International and participated in the club's charitable works. I also volunteered to participate in a local school district's

"Reach Out to Drop Outs" campaign. We formed small groups and knocked on doors to interact with as many high school dropouts as possible and encourage them to return to school. Some went to the school and registered that day.

So where does GoalMinds go from here? As we increase our resources and expand our product line, I want to focus more on the creative aspects of the business. Plans are underway for a program on BlogTalkRadio, more websites for our Take Charge of Your Life podcasts, and another book or two.

Where do you go from here? Follow your dreams. If it's a business of your own, learn what it takes.

Hold on to your security while making plans for that next step. Then step out and give it all you've got!

A Winning Attitude Makes a Difference

Joyce Robinson Agu, CBS's *Amazing Race* winner, shares her wonderful story of getting selected to be on one of America's favorite television shows. She also reveals how her experience of developing a different mindset and perspective on life helped her become the winner of season seven.

Joyce Robinson Agu Wins an Extraordinary Race: A Lesson in Humility, Faith, Perseverance, and Teamwork

How many of us can say that we won a contest and became a better person, physically, emotionally, and spiritually? For Joyce Robinson Agu and her husband Uchenna Agu, it was more than just a contest. Up to that point, it was the most challenging goal they had ever set for themselves. They were winners of CBS's *Amazing Race*, Season 7.

A daring spirit, risk-taking attitude, and the thrill of excitement inspired them to enter the contest. Patience, teamwork, faith, humility, understanding, and tolerance are what they learned during the contest. An unstoppable attitude is what they gained after winning. From being stripped of their finances and belongings to begging for money to pay cab fare, this team had a cohesive attitude and the determination to win. Do you have a winning attitude? What risks are you willing to take?

Agu enthusiastically talked about her life as an actress and shared her experience about getting on the show, being a contender in the contest, and receiving the ultimate prize as the winner.

Monica: You've had much success as an actress. Talk about some of the roles that you have taken and why you decided to play those roles. Did they lead to more successful roles?

Joyce: I've always considered myself to be a very creative person and acting was something I always wanted to do, even though Mom wanted me to go to school and get an education. But I did find some success in soap operas. I was actually on *The Bold and the Beautiful*, and at one point, this is how old I am, I was on a black soap opera called *Generations*. I had a recurring role on that show.

I got my acting career going a little bit later in life. I played a 16-year-old teenage girl in my first role, and it was great. It led me to other roles. I've done movies, such as *Coming to America* and *Demolition Man*. I also had a recurring role on *Star Trek: The Next Generation*.

It was a wonderful career, although I was never truly famous for acting. I decided to give it up when I got married and moved to Texas. I thought I would pursue another field and go in a different direction. I thought it was a great career at the time and it was fun while it lasted, but it was time to move on. Strangely enough, when the show *The Amazing Race* started, it brought me back to Hollywood.

Monica: What piqued your interest in *The Amazing Race*?

Joyce: When they were looking for people to be on the show, they were searching for people who wanted an adventure of a lifetime and would be able to travel around the world. When I saw it, I thought, "This would be amazing. This would be a really great way to travel around the world with someone else picking up the tab."

I thought this would be a trip of a lifetime. I didn't know that it would be the hardest thing I've ever done in my life. I thought it was going to be the most amazing thing. Little did I know how difficult it would be to get on the show, but it was the beauty of the places that they were going and the idea that I could fulfill an item on my bucket list.

Monica: What difficulties did you experience in trying to get on the show?

Joyce: It's funny because like so many things in life you have to show up. I remember thinking I wanted to be on the show but I had no idea how I was going to do that.

We ended up applying on three different occasions to three different shows. The first time we sent in the video and application, we never heard from them. The second time, we got through to the interview process. Once they interview you, they send you to Los Angeles to meet with network personnel for a two-week interview process.

At the end of the two weeks, they decide whether you're in or not. They sent us home at the end of the second week. We were out of luck and out of our vacation time from our jobs. So we applied one more time. Actually, they called us back and asked, "Are you still interested?"

At that point my husband was thinking, "I'm done with this. These people keep calling us back. We keep going through this process, and they don't pick us."

We went back a third time, and we had to appear before network executives so that they could assess our personality. It was a lengthy process, but the third time was the charm. It probably took us about a year and a half to actually get on the show.

Monica: What are the most unique challenges you encountered after you were selected for the show?

Joyce: The first challenge was the reality of the show. When you see the show on TV, it looks so fun because you take on really cool challenges at all these different locations around the world. But what you don't see is the time that it takes. Sometimes it could take 12 hours on a flight to get to the location. After you get to the location, you still have to go through the challenge. Some of the challenges can take up to eight hours. What you see on TV is maybe a couple of minutes or a few seconds.

The most difficult part is going to foreign countries and dealing with the cultural differences and the things that we, as Americans, take for granted. I never considered language barriers to be a problem until I had to ask for directions from someone who didn't speak English. We shouldn't expect it, but as Americans, we think that everyone should speak English.

Another challenge involved exchanging currencies. I remember being in some remote locations where some of the people had never seen American currency. If you haven't taken the time to exchange your currency while in their country, you're going to have difficulty making purchases and paying for services. They will not accept American currency.

Having to drive on the opposite side of the street was an additional challenge. In some countries, people don't want to speak with you if you have a camera in their faces. When they see cameras, they may associate that with government intervention or some other type of issue. They don't think like Americans when cameras are around, "Oh, this is fun. This is my chance to get on TV." People run away from the cameras and they don't want to be bothered.

Another thing that people don't know is that whenever you ask for directions or stop to try to talk to someone, your camera crew has to get that person's approval and a signed release form in order to be shown on TV. Everything has to be shown on TV because it shows your quest and the route you've taken to get where you are. Oftentimes there's a language barrier with the release form. They are hesitant to sign anything because some people think they're signing their lives away.

There are also mental and physical challenges. The objective is to get to the next stop without being eliminated. Usually, the last team gets eliminated. Occasionally, they do something called a fast-forward, which basically allows you to do something that they've conjured up. It's usually really physically or mentally tough, and if you complete this challenge, then you can usually skip the other challenges and go straight to the pit stop. Taking on this challenge often puts you in first place.

At one point, we decided to go for it because we had been coming in very close to last for most of the race at that point. We were in Jodhpur, India. We went to a location in India where we had to find a person who was sitting on the edge of a river in the mountains. And there he was sitting in front of a temple.

The challenge noted that in India, for good luck and good fortune, people will shave their heads once in their lifetime. In order to complete this task you must shave your head. That was my biggest fear ever. My husband was already bald, but all eyes were on me. Everyone was wondering what I was going to do because I not only had long hair, I had extensions. I had big hair.

The idea that I would shave my head for a TV show just horrified me, but I said, "Just do it. I'm not going to think about it anymore."

As soon as they began cutting my hair, my feelings were hurt. I kept thinking, "Wow, they could have started from the back. Maybe I could have changed my mind if I decided to do that." But they started right in the front with scissors, and before I knew it, everything had been chopped off. I was shiny and bald, just like my husband.

I thought about the saying, "For good fortune and good luck, people do this once in a lifetime." And then I thought, "Just relinquish all the ideals about who you are. It's just hair and you are more than just your hair. After my head was shaved, it had a strange effect on me.

Afterwards my husband said, "Wow, you suddenly became like a soldier. I've never seen you this way." I had never felt that strong before. I felt like I could do anything.

Monica: With the lesson you learned from that one experience in shaving your head, what inspirational message can you offer other women?

Joyce: I'd say that you can increase physical results through your mental fitness. You are mentally stronger than the exterior that you present to the world. I felt that I was no longer going to hide behind being a weak female. I felt that everything I am, I have to present to the world. There's no reason for you to live for other people's expectations. Why not be the powerful woman that I am? Who cares if it offends someone?

Some men are intimidated by strong women, but I personally use that to my advantage. I use that advantage because I want them to help me move ahead and get promoted. Sometimes, even with other women, you may feel intimidated because you don't want to offend people. But I thought, "Why do I care about other people's perception of me? If I'm living through their eyes, I'm not living up to my potential."

Be who you are with no apologies.

Monica: Compared to the challenges that you faced, how does that affect your views regarding the adversities experienced by the people in the countries you visited?

Joyce: When Americans go to other countries, we feel superior because some of the places we visit aren't as advanced as we are. It's so easy to say, "This sucks!" or "We have the best answer to everything." But what I realized is that in some countries they don't have the diseases and issues that we have. In America, we create so many issues that we develop other problems. So I learned to respect them and their cultures for what they are.

Monica: How has working together as husband and wife impacted your relationship?

Joyce: We are now divorced, but when we were on the show, we weren't sure if we were going to stay together. We had gone through the demise of the companies that we worked for. Our careers were crumbling, and we were trying to figure out how we were going to overcome our difficulties.

It affected our relationship a little bit, but when we were on the *Race*, it was really strange how amazingly perfectly we worked together. We respected each other, and we didn't blame each other for the choices that were made. It was almost like when you're at home, it's easy to be nitpicky about all the things that you have in your controlled world. But when we were experiencing new things together, we clung to each other. We looked to each other and thought, "Should we do this or shouldn't we do that?"

We had such camaraderie that people thought, "These guys are such a great couple." We felt that we could maintain this perfect partnership because we worked so well together. It really helped us move ahead in the game. Of course, when you return home, you return to your normal habits and creature comforts.

Monica: Near the end of the race, the two of you had to ask for money to pay the taxi driver. What was going through your mind at the time? Did you think someone else might win?

Joyce: Before we even got there, we still had a belief that we could win. We were traveling with a plastic bag with our passports, our medications, and no money. I can now really relate to people who have come from absolutely nothing. When they took that away, we thought, "OK, you're taking everything away, but you didn't take our brains and you didn't take our hearts."

It was difficult because the other teams were given about $250 and we had no money and had to travel from one point to another. It was about a 250-mile round trip and they were able to ride while we had to walk and find other means of travel.

We became very humble, thankful, and grateful because we had to rely on the kindness of others. We had to talk to people and appeal to their human side. That was the most humiliating thing. At one point, my husband offered his wedding ring. He was told, "I don't want your ring. I need cash. I've got to pay bills. I have a family." So we thought at that point we had a choice. We could have finished the race or we could stay there and try to earn the money. This was crazy because we didn't know whether we were first or last.

But we decided to stay there and attempt to beg for the money. One guy actually told us, "Begging ain't the way to do it, brother."

And that's where it became interesting for me. I developed a different viewpoint. Now when I see people begging on the streets, I wonder about their story. You never know what their story is. I knew people had no idea what my story was, but I couldn't explain why I needed cash. I remember there was a lady who was watching us from her apartment window above, and she must have been watching for a while. Any cars that pulled up, we'd try to get them to give us a couple of dollars.

The lady came down the stairs and she asked why we were raising funds. We couldn't disclose that we were doing a show, but we could tell her we were in a race. We said, "We're in a race, we can't pay our cab fare, and we need a few more dollars."

She gave us what we needed to pay the cab fare and it was awesome. When this lady showed up, it changed everything. Then we were able to run in, and we got there and we heard, "After 40,000 miles and 25 countries, you guys are the winners of the race." It was awesome!

It was the most amazing feeling ever because it was one of the first times where I felt that I had truly completed something. I stuck to my intentions, even though throughout the race there were many times when I thought, "I can't do this anymore. I can't go on. I want to quit. I want to stop because this is too painful and this is too hard. I am too hungry." I didn't like being broke, I didn't like being bald, I didn't like being dirty, and I didn't like the way people looked at me. I remember some people told our production personnel that we stunk.

At that point, I was bald and wearing a scarf on my head. I'm sure I looked more like a street person. It was very humbling. From the whole experience, I realized the things that you don't need in your life to be successful. We had nothing and we still managed through the kindness of others and good karma because we always tried to make sure that we didn't hurt people along the way.

All you need is your brain, your thoughts, your intentions, and your drive and desires. You would be surprised what you can come up with. It was a real testament to willpower and the power of your intentions. It was an awesome lesson.

Monica: How are you applying some of those lessons that you learned from the race to your life experiences today?

Joyce: I know all the things that I've learned and I know all the things that have made me successful. But somewhere along the way things like my relationship have changed. I haven't stayed with that belief. But now I am writing a book, and we're beginning to do motivational speaking. We are telling people how you can come from nowhere and have nothing, yet you can live in the present. You don't have to wait for another time to be happy. You don't have to wait to have a lot of stuff before you can be happy. I am becoming the person that I want to be. The Race taught me is to extend my beliefs, my imagination, and my knowledge. It has expanded my awareness.

Monica: It has opened up an entirely new world for you.

Joyce: It really has. You don't know what you don't know. Make it your business to learn what else is in your world. The world is so much larger than the little things that we ask for.

Monica: If you had to sum up your experience and what you gained from *The Amazing Race*, what would it be?

Joyce: I would say that my complete and total awareness in my small world expanded. I've gained a new appreciation for the world and for my life. I feel that the possibilities are endless.

My life is much more exciting now. I love traveling. I love considering the other possibilities that may be out there when you stretch your limits. I'm still growing. When you get to the end of your rope, when you reach your bottom, then obviously you need to do something different. You have to change your thought process. You have to try something outside of your comfort zone. At that point, you need to grow.

Sometimes we become focused on trying to resolve issues by using the same thought process that caused the problem. At that point, it's time to look at things differently. I think that's the time you have to say, "OK, I've got to step outside of my world. Read something, learn how others are doing things, or just talk to people." Sometimes we get stuck in our own way of doing things when there's outside information available that can help us.

Live fully and beyond your fears. I think that fears keep people stuck. I know that I still have fears, but sometimes you have to expose yourself and not be afraid to be uncomfortable. Comfort is overrated sometimes.

You've got to have a goal. You've got to have something that you're looking forward to and that you are aiming for. You don't always have to know the answers to how you're going to accomplish something. You just need to have the desire and the intent. Once you do, it's amazing how things will change. Have a plan and an intention. Whether you know how to achieve it or not, things will eventually change.

Striving for Excellence

Entrepreneur extraordinaire Carlene Altom, founder of Core MSO, LLC, shares her story of how she turned her adversities into a success story for herself and for other entrepreneurs. She is using her God-given talents to help medical practices thrive.

Integrity and Values Helped Her Earn a Six-Figure Income

As a teenager, Carlene Altom was faced with adversity that most young ladies could never imagine. However, this strengthened her resolve to overcome challenges and to live the best life that she can.

Self-education became Carlene's defense against adversity. Her determination and commitment to excellence have enabled her to become one of the country's most successful professionals in the health care industry.

Altom began working at the age of 15, and it helped her build on life lessons and establish an incomparable work ethic. At 19, she began managing a dental practice that truly set her on the path to amazing success, despite the obstacles she encountered. She enhanced her skills and used them to help others build wealth through their businesses. As a result, she created wealth for herself.

Today, she is the woman with the Midas touch in the health care industry. Her creative solutions to office management have helped many doctors move their practices from near collapse to multi-million-dollar entities. "I got tired of seeing so many doctors get taken advantage of from so many aspects of their practice simply because it's not their forte, or they did not have the time," Altom stated.

Her solutions to office management have proven to be golden, and her advice is sought by many practitioners in the medical field. Altom believes, "If we don't get a grip on all of the business aspects of health care, physicians will not be able to afford to practice and provide the health care we all deserve."

Partnering with four remarkable individuals, including Dr. Robert G. Anderson, she and her partners created Core MSO, LLC, a multi-service health organization. Teamwork and values are the key elements to building successful relationships in any business. Altom has applied these elements in a way that has allowed medical professionals to thrive in their practices. Altom excitedly shared with the publisher of *Exceptional People Magazine* her passion for making a positive impact on the health care industry.

Monica: You are a believer in self-education. What does self-education mean to you? And in what areas do you continue to educate yourself?

Carlene: I believe that surrounding yourself with the right team is very important. It was OK to identify what my weaknesses were, but it was more important for me to focus on my strengths. Then I surrounded myself with the right people, identified what their strengths were, and, hoped that their strengths would help me improve my weaknesses.

It's also keeping up with marketing, understanding who I am, and knowing who I work with. I'm constantly at Barnes and Noble, reading articles on team building and dealing with difficult people. I don't have to be the best person to understand coding and billing. That's not my expertise, but I have to be able to understand that it's not my area of expertise and identify the right person for the job.

My continuing education is about understanding people and teams, identifying areas of weakness, and creating action plans to solve such problems. I'm trying to educate the people that I work with on how important their strengths are. All of my self-education has been about all of that.

Monica: You started working at the age of 15, and I'm sure you have experienced amazing life lessons and work ethics. Why did you start working so early?

Carlene: My mother was a stroke patient. She had her first stroke when I was in the eighth grade and the money wasn't there. We went from a two-income family to a single-income family overnight. I think it took about five to seven years to actually get

Social Security support and disability. We also had some abuse in the home.

Everyone has a story, but it's what you do with that story that makes you successful in overcoming obstacles. I started working for McDonald's. I learned the value of being a good employee. You were not allowed to lean on the counter. You had to be constantly doing something and being productive. They held you accountable for that time. A friend of my step-grandfather owned that McDonald's. I was able to see that the people you work with can make or break the team, a practice, or a business.

If you didn't ask, "Do you want fries with that?" you affected their bottom line because there's a reason behind it. I learned early on to ask that question and to be constantly busy and productive. Those people were the ones that stood out and got promoted.

I moved away from home at the end of my junior year. I worked two jobs during that time just to support myself. Then I got on a plane to meet the father I hadn't seen since I was three years old. That lasted a couple of weeks.

Then I worked for a Chevrolet dealership and where I learned the importance of personality and how it can impact people. I was working 60 hours a week greeting people who came to buy cars. It was my job to connect with the customer. If I didn't connect with them, then I couldn't get them into the dealership to speak to a manager.

It was important to identify and learn how to communicate with people. I had to learn how to be excited and educate people about something without selling to them. I earned $3.45 an hour and $5.00 for every car that was sold. That was 1989.

The relationship I thought I was going to have with my father didn't work out, so I ended up being in a new state by myself. I still have conversations with my father. We talk about things such as gardening and things from which we have a common bond. I realize you can't pick and choose who your family members are, but you can pick and choose how they affect your life. I used the relationship I had with my father as an example of how I didn't want my family to be. I used it as a measuring tool for the type of person I would marry.

I now support my mother after all these years. She left her abusive marriage and the environment that I grew up in. I try to take those negative experiences and use them as opportunities. The best revenge you can have in life is to succeed. I don't mean in obtaining material things, but you can do that by overcoming obstacles.

Monica: At the age of 19, you began working as a manager for a dental practice. From that you have built a strong work ethic and a remarkable career for yourself. What are some life lessons you learned along the way that have enabled you to become the successful person that you are today?

Carlene: When I moved to Baton Rouge, I had to live in the state for a year before I could attend college. I was very fortunate to meet my boyfriend's family. My boyfriend's mother introduced me to her husband who owned a dental practice. After they tested me, I began working at the front desk for minimum wage at $4.25 per hour.

I would pull recall charts and read through them. I thoroughly studied the various services the patients had and analyzed how I could better run the office. For example, I saw that a patient who had deep fillings hadn't returned for a long while, and I thought, "Deep fillings can lead to root canals if they are not monitored." So, I created a need for such patients to come in to get their teeth cleaned.

When I contacted patients, I would talk to them about the services they had. I would tell them that by doing preventative services they would avoid future and larger problems from occurring. For each patient that came in, I received $5.00. I would test what worked and didn't work in terms of how I spoke to the patients.

I remember looking through a ledger and I saw whiteout. I thought, "That's a legal document. You can't put whiteout on legal documents." I had identified employee fraud. There were employees who were creating charges for their spouse's insurance that didn't exist, collecting money from it, and having it assigned to the family instead of to the doctors. It was really sad. Your team is the key to your success. If you have a bad team, your success will diminish. I noticed that doctors were being taken advantage of consistently from an employee standpoint.

I also worked for Liz Claiborne as one of the young ladies who would spray people with perfume as they walked by. I learned early on that the hardest thing to manage is accountability. When you're in a position where you're accountable and no one is directly over you, as a company you have to make sure that you have that right person in that position. I could tell the team had not been doing their job. I recommended to the representative that we beat the current goals, so we started doing events. In my little position, we were able to exceed the goals and set all new levels of expectations for all of their lines within the dealer's account across Liz Claiborne.

My boss at the time said to me, "You could sell ice cubes to an Eskimo." I told her I don't want to sell and she said, "When you just talked somebody who has no front teeth into pure perfume, that's selling."

At my father-in-law's dental practice, I had identified a lack of team building, initiative, and bad attitudes. By the time I was 26, I helped him triple his practice and identified debt on the books, When I uncovered that he was experiencing employee theft, he literally fired his entire team in one day.

I took off some time and I became a single mother. I experienced things that I tried to avoid from growing up, such as the violence in the home. During that time, I started a non-profit organization for working single moms. I identified that there were a lot of single mothers that had a stigma about looking for a father or someone to support them.

I thought to myself, "These are my mistakes and I don't want society to take care of them."

I wanted to find a way to take care of them myself. There was a time when my mother was on the system but that time had passed and we were off of it. Through the organization, I wanted to help single mothers become independent.

Monica: What advice can you impress upon young ladies today about living up to their potential even in their teenage years and why they should take advantage of the great opportunities that are available to them?

Carlene: Number one, I would say understand who you are first. Identify what's important to you. What are your core values? What do you want people to say about you when you're gone? Then picture in your head exactly what you want out of life. You don't have to have all of the details. Just have the big picture. Don't try to improve on your weaknesses, instead improve on your strengths. Don't focus on what you don't want. Focus on what you do want.

I didn't know how I was going do to it, but I just knew that when I turned 40, I was going to make six figures. I knew that I would weigh a certain amount and I'd look a certain way. I had the image in my head. I had to have a successful marriage. I put that image in my head when I was 25 years old, because I was overweight at that time and I was not in a good marriage. My ex-husband repeatedly told me things that would make a person not feel good about themselves. I decided to focus on what I wanted and it actually happened.

Monica: How do you maintain balance in your life as a mother, as a very successful career woman, and continue to educate yourself?

Carlene: I do it by trial and error. I try to listen to myself and what feels right. I cannot say that I have not missed things with my children or with work. It's very tricky when it comes to prioritization. I have a lot of support. I have a great husband. I have great team members that I work with at the practice with Dr. Anderson. I can't do it all myself. The only way that I can balance things is to have a good support team around me.

Monica: You have partnered with four outstanding individuals to create a company called Core MSO (Multi Service Organization). What is Core MSO and what are you accomplishing through the company?

Carlene: Core MSO was created because I felt doctors needed a place where all of the business aspects of running a medical practice such as team building, collections, billing, acquisition, credentialing, seminars, mergers, litigation, medical spas, and surgical centers could be under one roof.

We all have the same common goal to help our health care providers. We all provide a service, and we can come together under one company with the same core values, shared vision, and mission. It's never been done before on the medical side. Integrity, passion, and teamwork are our three main core values. Our clients' success is our success. I wanted to be able to help doctors. They need to be protected.

Monica: You have done an excellent job so far. I'm sure your clients are very appreciative of what you have done for them. Not only have you cleared out the corruption, the fraud, and the negativity, but you have helped many of them to build multi-million-dollar businesses.

Carlene: Thank you.

Important Information for Purchasers of This Book

This book can be purchased in bulk. If you or your business associates hold special events where you engage with entrepreneurs or small business owners throughout the year, *Welcome to the Top* would make an excellent gift.

Here are a few ideas on how *Welcome to the Top* could be offered to provide value to your market:

1. If you sell products to entrepreneurs and small business owners, host Small Business Saturday events, where they register for a one-hour workshop held in your store. The attendees could receive a free copy of *Welcome to the Top* for taking the workshop.

2. If you are a restaurant or coffee shop owner and want to bring more business people into your establishment, offer a special menu on a given day or promote an event throughout the week where the first 50 business owners or entrepreneurs that order from your lunch menu will receive a free copy of *Welcome to the Top*.

3. For a non-profit or for-profit association that serves the small business community, a great way to offer more value for your membership would be to give them a free copy of the book.

These are just a few ways you can use *Welcome to the Top* to bring added value to your customers, clients, or members. Not only that, but you will also be strengthening networks of local businesses and encouraging the support of each other, something that all small business owners and entrepreneurs can benefit from.

If you're interested in a bulk purchase of this book or you have relationships with others who could benefit from bulk purchases, contact Monica Davis at <u>monica@secretstosuccessbooks.com</u>.

Opportunities for Business Growth

Media Mastery

It can be hard when you're just getting started in your business or when you have a limited budget, and yet you know you need to quickly get in front of your audience.

Most successful business leaders and influencers have one thing in common. What sets them apart is their ability to spot opportunities in the media and use those to showcase their expertise. Successful business leaders use the media to present themselves as authorities with something to offer—and to stay in the minds of their audience.

It's critical that you get as much exposure for your business as possible without spending an enormous amount of time or money to do it. Publicity offers you a level of endorsement that no other form of marketing can. When you are endorsed by the media, it opens unlimited opportunities and gives you instant credibility. It positions you as an authority in your field and gives you much more leverage.

The **Media Mastery** program is a step-by-step comprehensive virtual learning program. It provides easy-to-implement formulas and specific strategies you can immediately put to work to get your name in front of your prospects with little or no cash outlay by harnessing the potency of the media.

If you want to learn exactly how to put the media to work for you day in and day out, without having to spend a dime on ads, you'll want to invest in this course.

If you want to go from Best Kept Secret to Industry Leader, visit https://training.exceptionalmediacoaching.com to learn more.

Increase Your Influence and Profits with Your Compelling Story

Is your brand's narrative pulling its weight?

Today's most powerful marketing revolves around a relatable, meaningful brand narrative. That's because buying decisions and customer loyalty are deeply influenced by the way you position your company's purpose and vision. People don't simply buy products or services; they buy into the principles, values, and the story behind your brand.

A well-developed brand narrative can separate and elevate you from your competitors as well as connect you with your ideal audience.

Your story goes where facts, figures, and analysis cannot: into people's hearts. A distinguishing story about you or your brand is one of the most memorable ways to establish connection and build a relatable persona.

Are you using your story to its fullest potential? We can help you transform your brand by crafting a provocative narrative. Your authentic narrative has the power to impact millions.

To learn more about Monica's "done for you" program, **Increase Influence and Profits with Your Compelling Story**, visit this page: https://exceptionalmediacoaching.com/your-story-equals-more-customers.

About the Author

Monica Davis is a business mentor, the founder of *Exceptional People Magazine*, an award-winning TV producer and host, media coach, and master communicator with over 21 years of experience in the media industry. She's helped hundreds of professionals, luminaries, entrepreneurs, and corporate leaders advance their mission and vision through compelling and unforgettable brand narratives and media insights.

Her company, Atela Productions, is the recipient of eight International Hermes Awards and has been named among industry-leading brands such as AARP, Deloitte, Fidelity Investments, Hilton, IBM, and Pepsi for conceiving, designing, and implementing innovative ways to brand, market, and communicate. She is also the author of *Start Your Business Right: A Comprehensive Guide to Entrepreneurship Success.*

Davis is available for coaching, training, webinars and other online events. To learn more about these opportunities, or share your interest in doing an event, contact Monica Davis at http://www.exceptionalmediacoaching.com/contact.

A Message from the Author

As you continue to pursue your entrepreneurial dream, I hope you are inspired by what you have read in this book.

I look forward to hearing from you and learning how *Welcome to the Top* may have helped change your perspective about how you run your business and the impact it has had on your life.

There are many teachable moments and lessons that were learned by these exceptional entrepreneurs and industry leaders. I believe these lessons can help you reach well beyond your goals to achieve extraordinary success.

If you have any questions or insights, or are interested in sharing your story, please email <u>monica@secretstosuccessbooks.com</u>. You can also write to me at Atela Productions, 2961-A Hunter Mill Road, PMB 624, Oakton, VA, 22124.

Any stories submitted by you may be used in future publications, though names may be changed to protect privacy. Due to the number of inquiries we receive, notification of receipt may not be possible.

Thank you for purchasing this book, and I wish you much success in your entrepreneurial endeavors.

With every wish for great achievements,

Monica Davis
703-273-2035
<u>monica@secretstosuccessbooks.com</u>

Your Action List . . .

Your Action List . . .

CPSIA information can be obtained
at www.ICGtesting.com
Printed in the USA
FSHW021552071020
74116FS